BE/BE
1st. Ed,

D1397284

INTERNATIONAL

SEAFOOD

by

Fisherman
LIBRARY

RECIPES

INTERNATIONAL
SEAFOOD
RECIPES

THE FISHERMAN LIBRARY
by Ocean Sport Fishing
1620 Beaver Dam Road
Point Pleasant, NJ 08742

© 1990, INTERNATIONAL SEAFOOD RECIPES

Published as part of THE FISHERMAN LIBRARY by Ocean Sport Fishing.

All rights reserved. No part of this book may be reproduced or utilized in any form or means, electrical or mechanical, including photocopying or recording, or by any information storage and retrieval systems without written permission of Ocean Sport Fishing.

Printed in the United States of America

Library of Congress Cataloging-in-Publication Data

ISBN 0-923155-10-4

THE FISHERMAN LIBRARY
Ocean Sport Fishing
1620 Beaver Dam Rd.
Point Pleasant, NJ 08742

Copy Editing . . . . Bob Rhodes
Production . . . . . . Captain Matt Muzslay
Art Direction . . . Steve and Terri Goione

ACKNOWLEDGEMENT...

I wish to extend special thanks to Mr. Pete Barrett and Mr. Matt Muzslay of OCEAN SPORT FISHING and Mr. Fred Golofaro of THE FISHERMAN'S LONG ISLAND EDITION for giving me the opportunity to share my collection of seafood recipes with my fellow fishermen.

And thanks to all the gracious folks who, over the years, furnished me with a wealth of recipes, cooking tips and general knowledge of fish cookery; my devoted wife, Dolores, my dear mother, Michelina; my precious grandmother, Luisa; Leonard Allen; Roger Allen; Sarah Ambrose; Edna and Harry Berman; Marjorie Burrell; Johnny Calamia; Daisy Cosme; Norma Cosme; Henry Derricco; Bobby Doshim; Eddie Garcia; Tony Green; Betty Harris; Carol Kum; David Kum; Harold Larish; Netty Lucas; Jean Luisi; Captain Paul Luisi; Maria Maccariello; Paul Nimeroff; Mary Ramirez; Artie Rose; Fred Schweers; Phil Sgueglia; Evelyn Shanley; Joseph "Smitty" Smith; Irma Valmer; Vincent Vigilante; Patricia Wright; Kin Ping Yip; Howie Yu; Gwen Ziegler; and Joe Zymblys.

INTRODUCTION...

A French cook once told me that to prepare authentic BOUILLABAISSE, you had to use fish not only native to the waters off the coast of France, but from a specific region, namely The Sea of Marseilles. Anything less would result in just another run-of-the-mill stew—and not BOUILLABAISSE!

Well, I wasn't about to rush out to the airport, hop on a jet for Europe, and gather fish in Southern France just so I could whip up a batch of BOUILLABAISSE in traditional fashion. Instead, I settled for local species, those native to the waters off the coast of Brooklyn, and put together a darn good "Yankee" version of the classic fish stew.

Of course, my purist friend was reluctant to admit that my efforts had produced true BOUILLABAISSE, yet that didn't stop him from making frequent trips to the steaming kettle of fish for refills.

That incident occurred more than twenty years ago and the success of its outcome had inspired me to tamper with another classic dish—GEFILTE FISH!

Traditionally, GEFILTE FISH, an old world Lithuanian dish, is prepared today as it had been for ages using freshwater species such as carp, whitefish, or pike, with few exceptions. I, being one who fishes almost exclusively in salt water, had little access to such sweet water species. So again I broke tradition and blended cod, blackfish, and flounder fillets to concoct a SEA-STYLE GEFILTE FISH I could be proud of.

Confident of the success of my achievement, I took a sample to a sweet, little Jewish lady who ran the neighborhood newsstand. Upon tasting the chilled fish dumplings I had prepared, she marvelled at the fact that I, one not of the same ethnic background commonly associated with preparing this dish, could come up with a finished product superior to the store-bought and comparable to the homemade versions of GEFILTE FISH.

When I confessed that I had used species of fish unfaithful to the original, rigidly adhered to, recipe, she became distressed. Not so much because I had substituted salt water fish for freshwater fish but whether or not the fish I had selected were kosher. She smiled, relieved, when I assured her they were.

BOUILLABAISSE and GEFILTE FISH are but two of the many seafood recipes featured in this book which smash the barriers of tradition and conformity and place such classic dishes within easy reach of the local angler. But above all, THE NORTHEAST SALT WATER FISHERMAN'S INTERNATIONAL COOKBOOK is a text geared to the fisherman, with the fisherman's interests at heart, and spoken in a language familiar to fishermen.

Chapter One discusses fully what the fisherman can, and should, do to ensure his catch maintains its freshness and quality from the rails of a fishing boat right to the kitchen table. Chapter Two provides detailed instructions on the many methods of cleaning and preparing your catch from pan dressing to boning a whole fish. And if your day's catch outweighs your needs for the night's supper, this chapter guides you through preparing your surplus catch for the freezer.

Then before you suit up with apron and chef's hat in preparation for one of the exotic dishes featured in this book, Chapter Three introduces you to the fundamentals of fish cookery.

The remaining chapters escort you on a culinary voyage through many lands, into many cultures, featuring native dishes from plain to fancy, from simple to elaborate, from classical to contemporary, using those species of marine life familiar to and easily obtained by The Northeast Salt Water Fisherman!

TABLE OF CONTENTS

CHAPTER 1

FRESH FISH! FRESH FISH!

by
AGLIANO

Sal

1

Sal

FRESH FISH! FRESH FISH!

Nothing is more crucial to the success of a well-planned seafood dinner than the freshness of the fish used to prepare the meal. And without a doubt, the angler who catches his own supper has the best possible guarantee that fish destined for the dinner table will be fresh. But even under such ideal conditions, freshly caught fish can deteriorate rapidly if you fail to exercise the utmost care in handling your catch.

Fish flesh is highly perishable. Decomposition begins almost immediately after death with the greatest concentration of bacterial growth developing in the digestive system at an alarming rate. Gutting each fish soon after capture will certainly slow down the decaying process; however, this worthy precaution is only a halfway measure and quite often gutting each fish immediately after it's caught is not practical. The most effective method of retarding bacterial action is to immediately place your catch on ice, maintaining a temperature as close to just above freezing as possible. And if you can take the time to gut your catch as well as keeping it iced—all the better!

But how do you keep a mess of fish cold enough to prevent spoilage while fishing aboard a boat or along a stretch of beach, especially with the sun beating down at ninety degrees or better? One solution is to invest a few bucks in a heavy-duty, well insulated plastic or aluminum cooler. Sufficiently iced, a cooler will keep your catch cold (and fresh) for hours.

Although there are a multitude of these portable ice chests available in many shapes and sizes, not all fit the needs of an active fisherman. Select a cooler with a well-seated, tight-fitting cover. Inspect the hinges and locking mechanism. All hardware should be of a non-corrosive material such as copper, brass, aluminum, or stainless steel. Also check to see that the cooler is equipped with a functioning drain. This will make it easy for you to rid the cooler of excess water as the ice melts. Above all, choose a cooler that will fit all your fishing needs, taking into consideration the size as well as the number of fish you expect your cooler to accommodate.

For maximum efficiency, wait until the last possible moment before setting up your cooler. There are several freezing agents that can be introduced into your cooler. The most effective is dry ice, yet this form is not easily obtained and caution must be exercised in keeping your catch from direct contact with dry ice. This can be accomplished by placing several layers of cloth (terry cloth works splendidly) over the ice to form a barrier between your catch and the dry ice.

If dry ice is hard to come by, you can use crushed ice or ice cubes. Pack at least six inches of ice into the bottom of the cooler, then cover the ice with layers of cloth. The cloth forms a barrier as it also absorbs much of the melted ice water. But because of a greater surface area, crushed or cubed ice will melt much faster than a solid block of ice. Block ice, on the other hand, is cumbersome to handle and takes up a great deal of precious space in the cooler.

Some innovative anglers avoid such problems by lining their coolers with several water-filled frozen milk cartons. When fit snugly in the bottom of a cooler, these miniature ice blocks will melt more slowly than crushed or cubed ice and will not take up as much room as the standard size block of ice. To work effectively, however, the cartons must be frozen solid, not slushy. So begin freezing the cartons of water at least 24 hours before a planned fishing trip.

If the idea of frozen milk cartons interests you, but you'd rather not bother with the extra work involved, consider manufactured ice packs sealed with freezing liquid. These can be washed after each trip, refrozen, and used many times over.

While fishing keep your cooler out of direct sunlight. Open the lid only to deposit fish as they are caught. Nevertheless, expect ice to melt during the course of the day. To prevent your catch from becoming water-logged, periodically drain the excess water by removing the drain plug or opening the drain valve and tipping the cooler until the water runs off.

To keep your cooler in tip-top shape, after each trip scrub it thoroughly inside and out with a solution of warm water and a mild detergent. If, after cleaning, a foul smell persists, fill the cooler with cold water and stir in about a cup of baking soda. Let it stand for at least one hour, then rinse the cooler and turn it upside down to dry. Properly cared for, your cooler will provide many years of useful service.

If a cooler is not practical for your style of fishing, have no fear, a clean burlap sack will provide an alternate method of preserving your catch. Keep the sack wet, douse it frequently and liberally with fresh sea water, and your catch will be as fresh several hours later when you're ready to prepare dinner as when it was caught.

Most frequently used, especially by party boat fishermen, are five- and seven-gallon plastic buckets joint compound or industrial soaps come in. Yet widespread misuse of these handy containers has turned many a decent catch into a slimy mess unfit for human consumption. One of the greatest sins committed afloat by novices and (sorry to say) experienced fishermen alike is to drop live, frisky fish into a bucket filled with sea water with no thought about changing the water frequently. Fish not only die quickly due to a diminishing supply of oxygen, but the water increasingly warms to the temperature of the surrounding atmosphere, which encourages bacterial growth. Better to cover your catch with wet cloths which are wrung out from time to time and replenished with fresh sea water.

On cooler days (with temperatures below 45 degrees), a plastic bucket can easily be converted into a make-shift cooler. Set up the bucket with ice and layers of cloth just as you would a cooler. Keep the cover on tight, position the bucket out of direct sunlight, and your catch will remain fresh for many hours.

Skiff and pier fishermen have the best advantage for keeping their catch not only fresh throughout the day, but alive! This can be accomplished by depositing your catch in an overboard live fish box, where fresh sea water is constantly flowing. Of course, you're not going to find any of these contraptions in a tackle shop or sporting goods store, but any angler with a minimum of carpentry skills and a free afternoon can construct a workable fish box. The box can be as simple or as fancy as you want as long as it does the job. I once put together a crudely constructed fish box out of an old vegetable crate into which I wedged chicken wire. Primitive? Yes! But it served me well for two seasons of active pier fishing.

But if you're of a mind to construct something more durable and less in the fashion of Huckleberry Finn, the following fish box plans should be of some help. You will need four panels of 1x12-inch pine shelving (two 18 inches long, two 8 inches long), four 1x¾-inch pine strips (two 20 inches long, two 6 inches long), one sheet of chicken wire measuring 8x20 inches, and about 4 dozen 1½-inch brass wood screws.

Arrange the pine shelving into a box frame measuring 8x20 inches. Using about six brass screws for each corner, secure the 8-inch end panels to the 18-inch side panels. Spread the chicken wire tightly and evenly over the box frame, then place the pine strips over the chicken wire and align with the box frame. Secure the pine strips to the box frame with brass screws spaced about two inches apart. This will hold the chicken wire in place. Trim off with wire cutters any wire that protrudes from the box.

If you wish, you can rig a cover with a sheet of ¼-inch plywood and two brass cabinet hinges. Cut the plywood to the exact dimensions of the top of the fish box. If you decide to mount handles and a locking mechanism, these should be made of non-corrosive material such as copper, brass, aluminum or stainless steel.

When finished, apply two coats of marine paint over the entire surface of the fish box, including the hardware and chicken wire. This will help preserve your fish box, prolonging its life for many years of service.

All fishermen, at one time or another, experience a bad day on the water. Whether it be the wind, the tide, a poor choice of fishing grounds, or just fish that won't bite, the phenomenon does happen! Sometimes this slump extends over several weeks, and as a result we find ourselves shopping in the local fish market to satisfy our desire to eat fish. But how can we be sure the fish we purchase are as fresh and wholesome as if we had just caught them?

A careful inspection will quickly separate those fish which are truly fresh from those which are not. The first order of business is to bring the fish up to your nose and sniff it. Yes, take a good whiff! If it smells as if someone had just opened a can of cat food, reject it! That fish has already begun to spoil. Contrary to popular belief, a fresh fish will not smell fishy or offensive; it will have a mild, almost sweet aroma.

Next, check the eyes, scales, gills, and fins. The eyes should be bulging and sparkling bright, not sunken and dull looking. Eye to eye, a fresh fish will look almost as if it were still alive. The scales should be tightly embedded in the skin, brightly colored with a slight sheen. The gills should be bright red to soft pink, not dull brown or fading gray. The gills of a spoiled fish will also smell badly. The fins should be firm not limp and show no signs of rot or discoloration.

OVERBOARD LIVE FISH BOX

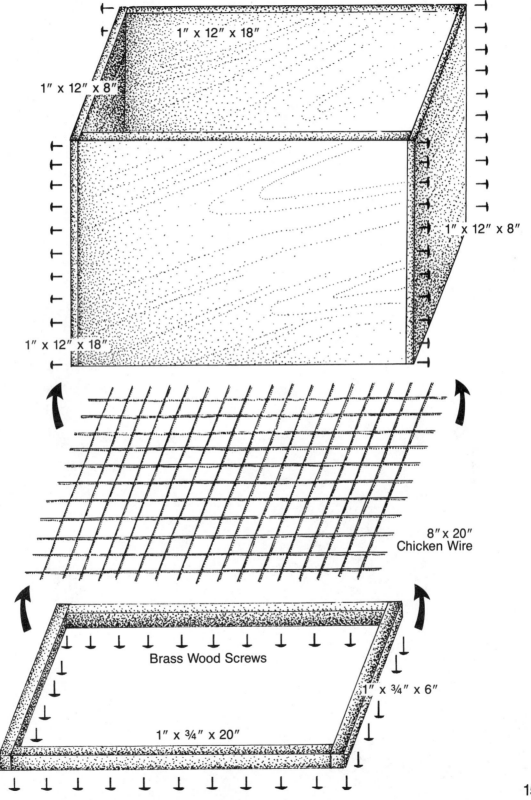

1" x 12" x 18"

1" x 12" x 8"

1" x 12" x 8"

1" x 12" x 18"

8" x 20"
Chicken Wire

Brass Wood Screws

1" x ¾" x 6"

1" x ¾" x 20"

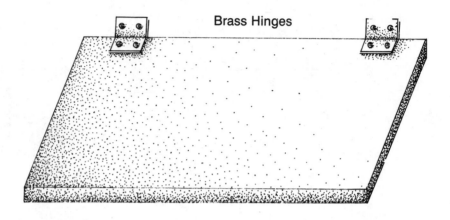

Brass Hinges

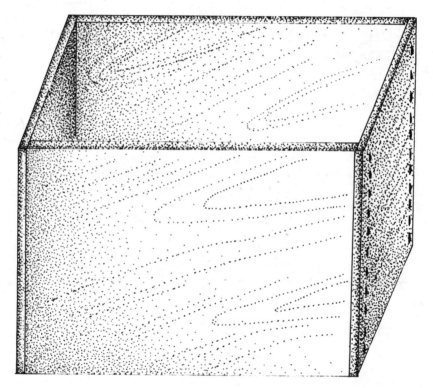

Finally, check the fish's body. A fresh fish will be firm and elastic. Test by pressing your finger into the flesh. If it springs back, it's a good sign that the fish is fresh. If an indentation remains, the fish is beyond prime condition.

Follow these guidelines when purchasing fish, and don't hestitate to reject that which fails the test of freshness. If the fish peddler refuses to allow you to inspect his goods, find another place to shop!

To further ensure the success of your seafood dinner, whether the fish are purchased from the market or taken directly from the sea, begin cleaning and preparing the fish as soon as you arrive home.

CHAPTER 2

THE ART OF CLEANING FISH

by AGLIANO

Sal

2

THE ART OF CLEANING FISH

If you ever wanted to closely observe a truly skilled craftsman in the art of cleaning and preparing fish, you need look no further than the stern of a busy party boat homeward bound after a day's fishing. With surgeon-like skill and super human speed an experienced mate will usually render a boat load of fish into table fare in less time than it takes to return to port.

What makes these individuals so proficient in the art of cleaning fish? I can answer in one word: practice! I recall the very first time I attempted to fillet fish some thirty odd years ago. After hacking away for the better part of an hour at a meager haul of flounders, I ended up with tattered sheets of fish flesh which looked as if they had been run through an office paper shredder. But with later attempts and increased confidence, my skill increased. Today I can slice a mess of fish with as much accuracy as a party boat mate, although not with the same lightning speed.

Before attempting to clean fish, assemble the necessary tools to perform efficiently. Usually all you will need is a long, flexible boning knife and a professional fish scaler. However, several other tools should be considered. A butcher's saw comes in

ANATOMY HIGHLIGHTS

1. dorsal fin
2. pectoral fin
3. pelvic fin
4. anal fin
5. gill cover
6. lateral line

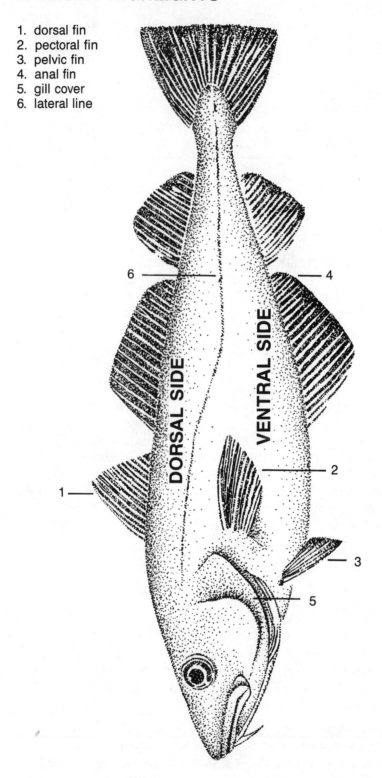

handy when cutting through thick bones. This tool is nothing more than a hack saw equipped with a stainless steel blade. Also a pair of heavy shears make removal of fins (other than the stubborn dorsal fin) a snap. And for shucking shellfish, nothing beats a clamming knife—a short thin tool with a rounded end, which resembles an over-sized butter knife. For maximum performance, keep all cutting tools razor sharp and free of nicks.

Set up a suitable work area with enough elbow room to operate comfortably, preferably near a sink and at waist level. The surface for cleaning fish should be flat—a slab of butcher block works exceptionally well.

Equally important are sensible work habits which will minimize the time spent cleaning fish. First, never keep more fish than you intend on using within a reasonable length of time. And throw back the shorties! It makes little sense to lug home more fish than you can possibly use, and it makes even less sense to keep fish so small they become a nuisance to clean while offering very little for the frypan.

Second, avoid unnecessary steps. If you plan on skinning your catch, don't bother to scale the fish. Not only is it a waste of time, but the scales provide rigidity which makes the skinning process much easier. Also, although it is advisable to gut your catch soon after capture, don't bother with it later if you are planning to filet the fish immediately upon arriving home.

Finally, perform one function at a time with all fish caught. For example, scale all the fish at one time, then fillet or gut them. A great deal of time is wasted scaling, gutting, and cleaning one fish before moving to the next.

SCALING

Embedded in the skin of most fin fish are protective plates called scales. If you prefer to cook fish in its skin, you must first remove the scales. This should be done before dressing or filleting, and when possible even before gutting.

To scale a fish, grasp it firmly by the tail, angle the scaler toward the head and scrape along the body in the direction of the head using short, firm strokes. When both sides have been done, rinse thoroughly under cold water to remove any loose scales.

FISH CUTS

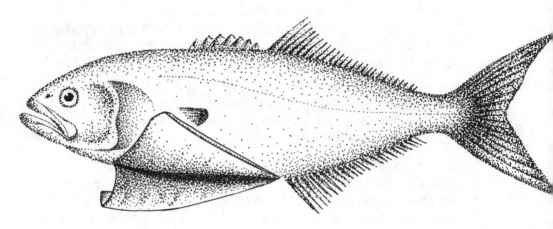

Whole (Gutted with gills removed)

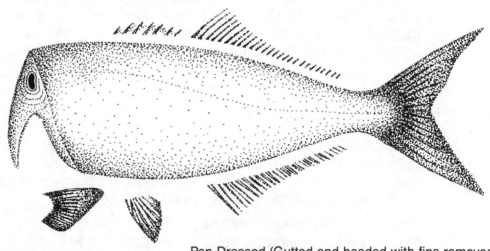

Pan Dressed (Gutted and headed with fins removed)

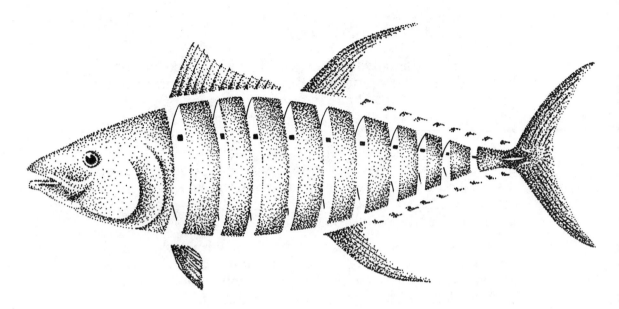

Steaks (Cross-section cuts from rib to tail)

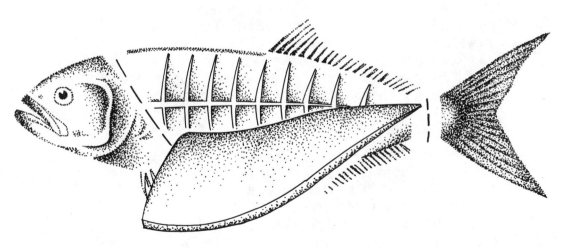

Fillets (Boneless flesh cut from both sides)

PAN DRESSING

Pan dressing is about the easiest and fastest method for cleaning fish, and with a little practice, you could dress a whole fish with but two strokes of the knife in a matter of seconds. Here's how it's done: push the point of the knife completely through the fish at a point just behind the pectoral fin. Angle the knife toward the anal opening and make a clean diagonal cut to the vent. Turn the fish belly-side up and cut downward from the original point of entry thus removing the head and the attached entrails in one continuous mass. You may remove the tail if you wish by simply cutting it away at the base.

If you prefer to cook the fish in its natural form—with the head and tail intact—you need only gut the fish and remove its bitter-tasting gills. Beginning at the anal opening, make a straight clean cut along the fish's underside from the vent to just beyond the gill opening. Reach into the gut cavity and remove the viscera. With the point of the knife, score along both sides of the backbone to open any blood pockets and release blood. Place the knife into the gill opening and sever the connecting tissue at the base of the head, then remove the gills. Rinse thoroughly inside and out.

A variation of this method will permit you to gut and remove the gills without cutting into the fish's underside. This method provides a pocket suitable for stuffing. Starting with a whole, scaled, but ungutted fish, insert a knife into the gill opening and sever the connecting tissue. Reach in and gently pull out the gills, the viscera should follow in a continuous mass. Probe your fingers to feel for any remaining viscera and squeeze it out by pushing on the underside of the fish toward the opening. Rinse thoroughly.

Pan dressed fish may be cooked with or without their fins. If you wish to remove the fins, do so just after scaling and prior to cutting into the fish. The pelvic, anal, and pectoral fins can be snipped off with kitchen shears. It is not advisable, however, to use shears to remove the dorsal fin as it is difficult to reach the root bones and many splinters may remain in the flesh. To remove the dorsal fin, make a deep cut along each side of the fin from head to tail and angled slightly inward toward the base of the fin. When done, grasp the fin with a cloth at the tail end and pull forward in one motion.

PAN DRESSING

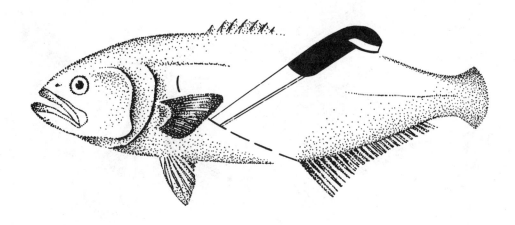

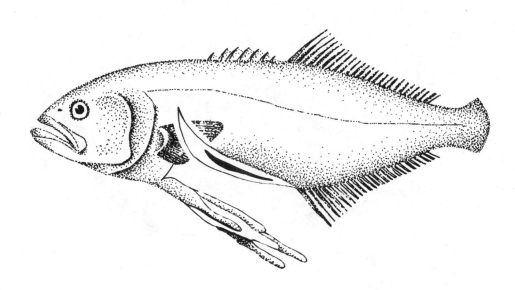

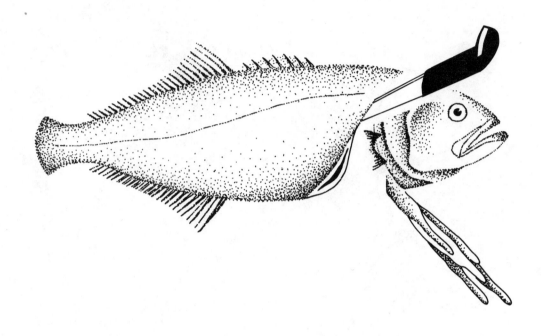

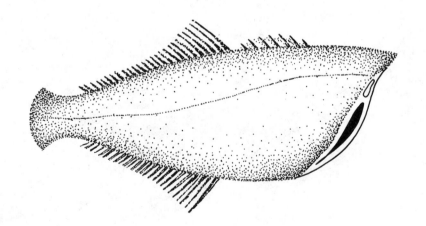

STEAKING

Roundfish of at least eighteen inches in length are best suited for steaking. Although this method is usually not practical for average-sized flatfish, teen-sized fluke can be steaked with satisfactory results.

To steak a roundfish, first scale and pan dress the fish. Turn the fish onto its belly and make several cuts about 1½ inches apart along the back, starting at the shoulder and finishing at the base of the tail. Cut only to the backbone. Next, turn the fish on its side and with a butcher's saw cut through the backbone at each interval. Follow through to the underside of the fish until each steak is cut away from the body. Leave the skin on; this helps to retain moisture and to keep the flesh from breaking apart. To steak oversized flatfish, follow the foregoing directions except keep the fish belly-side down through each step.

A medallion, often used in fancy dishes, is a cross-section of fish free of bones. A fish steak can be transformed into a medallion by carefully trimming away the central bone, then tucking the flaps into the space made by removing the bone.

FILLETING

Although filleting fish takes a great deal more time and skill than pan dressing and steaking, the final product is a clean piece of meat free of bone and usually skin. In some dishes, the skin is left on the fillet, in which case the fish must be scaled before filleting.

Pan dressed fish can be filleted; however, you needn't dress fish to fillet. Roundfish and flatfish are filleted in much the same manner, but because of a more uniform bone structure, flatfish are less troublesome. When filleting a whole fish, begin at the shoulder and make a diagonal cut to the vent just deep enough to reach the backbone. Make an additional cut across the base of the tail. This will produce a thin flap of flesh which should be pulled back gently as you continue to fillet. Make repeated strokes across the backbone from shoulder to tail until you've reached the underside of the fish and have freed a whole section of fish—a fillet! Turn the fish over and repeat the procedure on the opposite side. This method will produce two fillets.

FILLETING (METHOD #1)

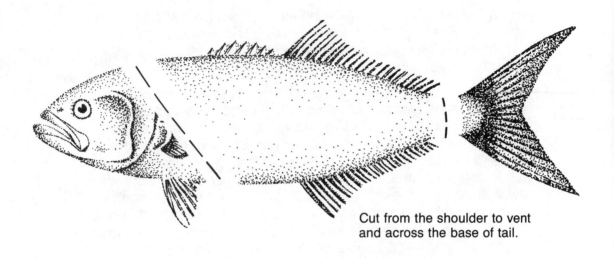

Cut from the shoulder to vent
and across the base of tail.

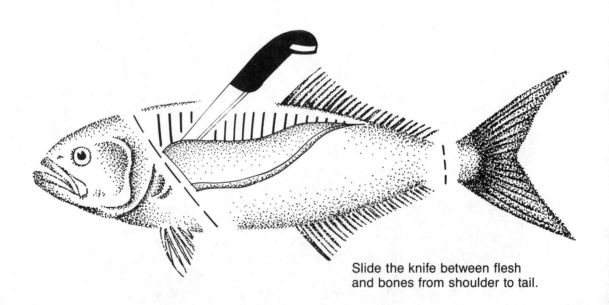

Slide the knife between flesh
and bones from shoulder to tail.

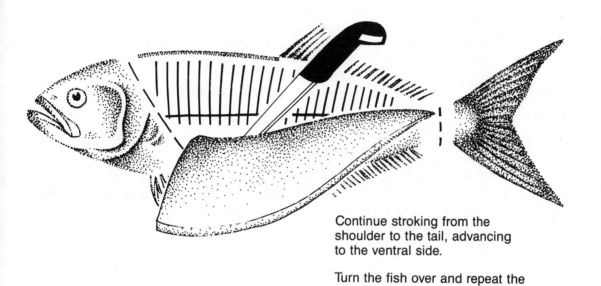

Continue stroking from the
shoulder to the tail, advancing
to the ventral side.

Turn the fish over and repeat the
same steps on the opposite side.

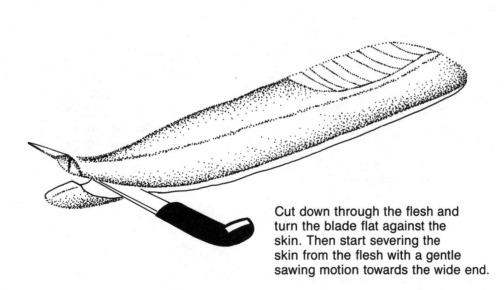

Cut down through the flesh and
turn the blade flat against the
skin. Then start severing the
skin from the flesh with a gentle
sawing motion towards the wide end.

Large fluke may be divided into four fillets by varying the above method. Make the same preliminary cuts from shoulder to vent and across the base of the tail. Then make an additional incision along the lateral line connecting the shoulder and tail cuts. Now, instead of filleting from the dorsal side to the ventral side, begin at the center and fillet out to the fins, first to the dorsal side then to the ventral side. Flip the fish over and repeat on the opposite side.

SKINNING

When skinning a whole roundfish, slit the skin across the body just behind the pectoral fin from shoulder to the pelvic area. Also slit across the base of the tail. Use the tip of a knife to pry up a snip of skin at the shoulder. Grasp the snip of skin with a cloth, then while holding the head down firmly, pull the skin to the tail cut. Repeat on the opposite side.

Here's a nifty maneuver that will allow you to skin a whole flatfish in one continuous motion. At the base of the tail slit the skin completely around. Lay the fish dark-side-up and pry up the skin at the tail with the tip of a knife. Hold the tail down firmly and pull the skin up and over the head. Flip the fish over, belly-side-up, hold down the head and continue to peel off the skin down to the tail.

When skinning pan dressed fish, make a small cut at the shoulder just under the skin. Grasp the snip of skin with a cloth, hold down the body and pull the skin toward the tail end. Repeat on the opposite side.

To skin fillets, lay the fillet skin side down on a flat surface. Make a cut about ½ inch up from the narrow end; don't cut through the skin. Hold this snip of flesh firmly with a cloth, angle the knife toward the wide end against the flesh, then pull the snip of skin in a back and forth motion while maintaining pressure with the knife. The fillet will roll upon itself until free of skin.

BONING A WHOLE FISH

If, like myself, you enjoy eating whole fish, but hate picking through bones, this preparation method makes seafood dining an absolute pleasure. Not only does the fish maintain its shape and natural beauty right to the dinner table, but the finished product is void of bones (except for the head and tail).

FILLETING (METHOD #2)

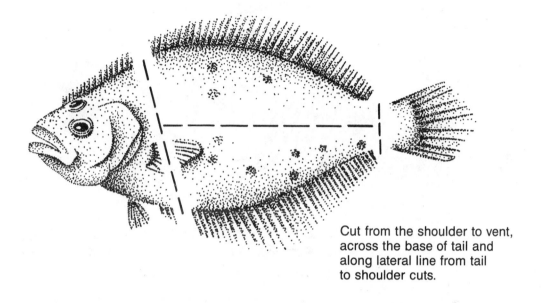

Cut from the shoulder to vent,
across the base of tail and
along lateral line from tail
to shoulder cuts.

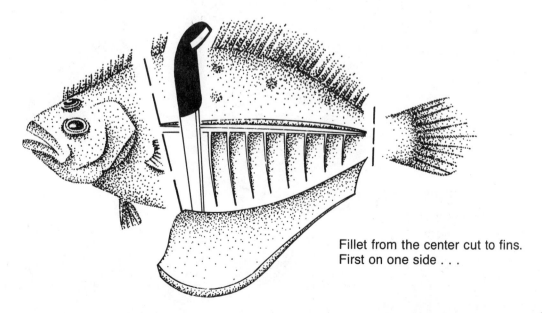

Fillet from the center cut to fins.
First on one side . . .

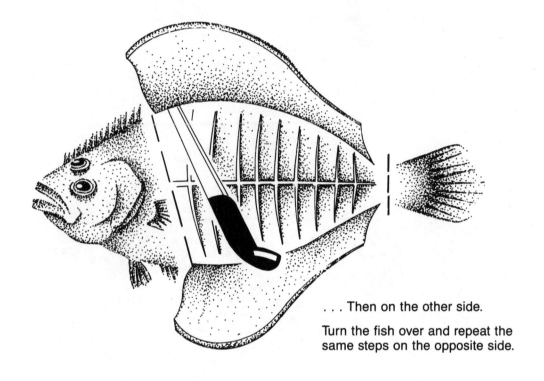

. . . Then on the other side.

Turn the fish over and repeat the same steps on the opposite side.

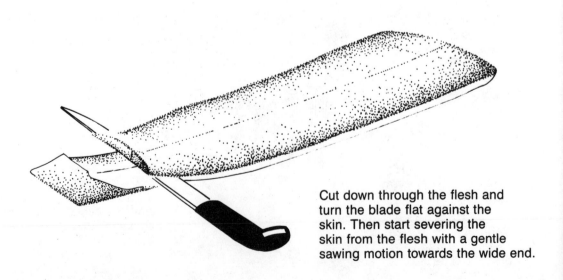

Cut down through the flesh and turn the blade flat against the skin. Then start severing the skin from the flesh with a gentle sawing motion towards the wide end.

The fish may be baked or broiled as is, or it may be stuffed, sutured with roasting cord, and baked.

Select any firm roundfish of at least three pounds (weakfish, sea bass, blackfish, bluefish, etc.). Scale the fish and remove its fins. Then gut and remove the gills. With a sharp knife, peel away the gut cavity membrane and score the blood pockets along the backbone. Slide your finger along the backbone until you feel the first rib bone, the one nearest the head. Gently insert the tip of the knife under and behind the first rib at the point connected to the backbone. Carefully slide the knife up along the rib bone and away from the backbone until the rib is free of flesh. Snip off the rib bone at the base of the backbone. Continue down the line from head to tail on both sides of the backbone, freeing each rib. Make shallow cuts along the sides of the backbone, snip the backbone at the head and tail with shears, then gently pull it out in one piece. Feel around for any stray splinters of bone lodged in the flesh and pluck them out with tweezers. Rinse thoroughly inside and out.

CODFISH IN FOUR PARTS

This method may sound like the title of an off-Broadway play, but actually it's a technique I use to get the most out of an oversized fish. Large codfish are main targets!

After gutting and removing the fish's fins and gills, divide the fish into four parts: head, tail rib section, and tail section. The rib section is cut into steaks, the tail section into fillets, and the head, tail, fins, and remaining skeletal frame set aside as a base for stock.

SKINNING AND DRESSING EELS

When I was a young squirt growing up in South Brooklyn during the fifties, there lived in the neighborhood an old fisherman named Sam Chiarmonte, who had a sure-fire method for skinning eels. He would drive a spike through the eel's head, mounting it to a huge old oak tree which stood in Sam's backyard. Although the eel had been killed instantly, it continued to quiver and twist for several minutes. Soon these post-mortem reflexes

DRESSING LARGE FISH

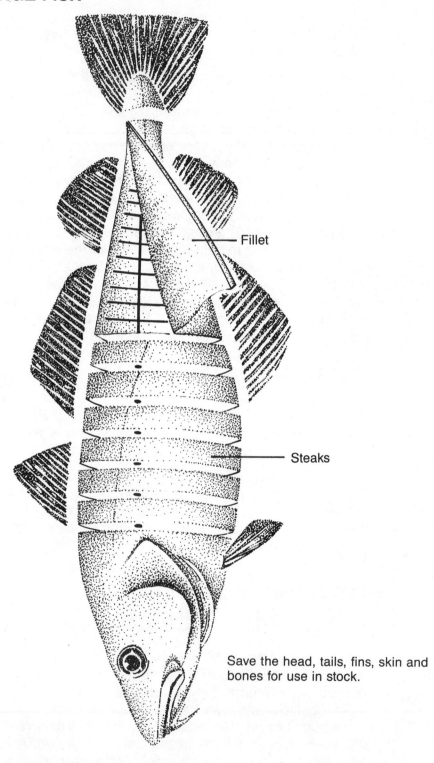

Fillet

Steaks

Save the head, tails, fins, skin and bones for use in stock.

subsided and Sam would make a slit completely around the eel just below the head. Then armed with two pliers, he yanked off the skin. Still dangling from the tree, the eel was gutted and beheaded. What Sam did with the remaining head and entrails is still a mystery, although I suspect he used them to fertilize his impressive vegetable garden.

Although this method circumvented the problem of trying to skin an eel as it wrapped and twisted around your arm in coils, it seemed to me a bit barbaric, to say the least. To dress an eel in a more civilized manner, firmly grasp the eel behind the gills and with one swift blow, strike its head with a heavy mallet, killing or stunning the snake-like fish. With a sharp knife, sever the head completely, then make a slit from the vent and remove the entrails. Pierce the knife at the shoulder to produce a snip of skin and flesh. Hold the body down firmly with one hand and with the other hand equipped with a cloth or pliers, pull the skin down along the body.

CLEANING (BLUE CLAW) CRABS

Whether captured in a crab trap, scraped off a piling, or purchased in the local fish market, crabs must be kept alive right up to the moment you begin cleaning to maintain flavor and freshness. When ready, each crab is instantly and mercifully killed either by driving a knife blade through the shell behind the eyes or plunging it into boiling water. Steamed crabs die slowly and due to my undying commitment to humane methods of slaughter, I shun the practice. Crabs, however, may be steamed after killing.

To kill crabs by boiling, set up enough kettles to accommodate your catch, each filled three-quarters of the way with cold water. I allow one 4-quart kettle for every six crabs. Place the kettle over high heat and when the water boils rapidly, plunge the live crabs into the boiling water (the crabs will die instantly) and boil for fifteen minutes. Don't become alarmed if the bubbling subsides momentarily. Usually when cold crabs are introduced into the water they lower the temperature temporarily. The bubbling should resume within moments.

Drain the boiled crabs in the sink and run cold water over them. When the crabs have cooled enough for handling, pry up the apron flap on the underside of the each crab and snip if off at the base of the top shell (in females this flap is triangular-shaped; in males it is T-shaped). Slip your fingers under the top shell and lift it off. Scrape out the spongy material located in the center chamber and pull off the finger-like gills along the sides. Rinse thoroughly. Some debris may be trapped in the crevices along the underside of the crab or in the claw joints. This can be removed by gently scrubbing with a fiber brush.

To kill crabs by stabbing, grasp the crab firmly at the back and insert the point of the knife forcibly into the crab's back just behind the eyes. This will kill the crab instantly. Follow the same procedure used for cleaning boiled crabs. A word of caution: blue crabs are frisky little devils even when sedated by mounds of ice. So when handling live crabs keep your fingers out of range of their powerful claws.

To kill soft shell crabs, cut across the body just behind the eyes with heavy shears. Reach into the crab area and remove the spongy material. Turn the crab over and snip off the apron flap. Turn the crab over again and gently lift to center the tapered point of the top shell, first on one side then the other, each time scraping out the gills. All remaining parts of the crab are edible including the back shell.

CLEANING LOBSTERS

Lobsters are prepared in much the same manner as crabs and should also be kept alive until cleaning. To stab kill a lobster, hold the animal right side up and drive the tip of a knife, with the sharp side facing the tail, completely through the back shell, flesh, and underside at the center of the lobster's back midway between the head and the top of the tail. Continue to cut through the lobster just to where the tail begins. Withdraw the knife and position it the opposite way so the blade is facing the head. Now, cut through to the head. If done correctly, the lobster should split right to the tail, with the tail section untouched at this point.

Turn the lobster over and using heavy shears cut through the undershell right up the middle from the tip of the tail to where the body is cut. Sever the tail from the body and remove the intestinal vein which runs the length of the tail. The tail may be left whole or cut into sections. Split the upper body in half and locate the gravel sac near the head; remove and discard the sac and the remainder of the intestinal vein. You will also find a greenish gray mass, the lobster's liver (or tomalley) and, in some females, dark green to black roe. Both tomalley and roe are located in the center chamber. These are edible and may be spooned out and used to flavor sauces.

Boil kill a lobster by plunging it head first into rapidly boiling water. Boil for about ten minutes. Drain and run under cold water. After the lobster has cooled enough for handling, clean it by the same methods as described for stab killed lobsters.

To remove cooked meat, break the lobster into sections and pick out the meat from one section at a time. The claws may be cracked open with a nut cracker or cut open with heavy shears and the meat picked out with a nut pick, a device resembling a dentist's tool.

CLEANING SHRIMP

Most of the shrimp's body is its tail. To clean, you need only remove the head, shell, and intestinal vein. Begin by grasping the head and twisting it off. Next, run your finger under the legs and shell and around the shrimp. Grasp the exposed meat with your hand and continue to peel around the shrimp down to the tail. Sections of the shell may break off. The tail shell may be left on, but if you'd rather remove it, just pinch it off. Make a shallow slit along the back of the shrimp to expose a dark thread-like vein. This is the intestinal, or sand, vein and can be pried up with the tip of a knife, lifted out and discarded.

To butterfly a shrimp, deepen the cut to remove the vein, then spread out the shrimp slightly with the palm of your hand. With the flat side of a broad knife, whack the shrimp very gently to flatten.

SHUCKING CLAMS AND MUSSELS

Before opening clams or mussels they should be scrubbed vigoriously of debris with a plastic or fiber brush under cold running water. Mussels must also be debearded by pulling out the thread-like hairs emerging from the shell.

To open, place the clam or mussel in your hand, the hinge-side resting in your palm. Slide the blade of the clamming knife between the shell halves on the side opposite the hinge and run the knife around the clam or mussel. Twist the blade slightly to separate the shell halves, then snap off the top shell. Slide the knife under the meat to sever the muscle attached to the bottom shell.

SECTIONING SQUID

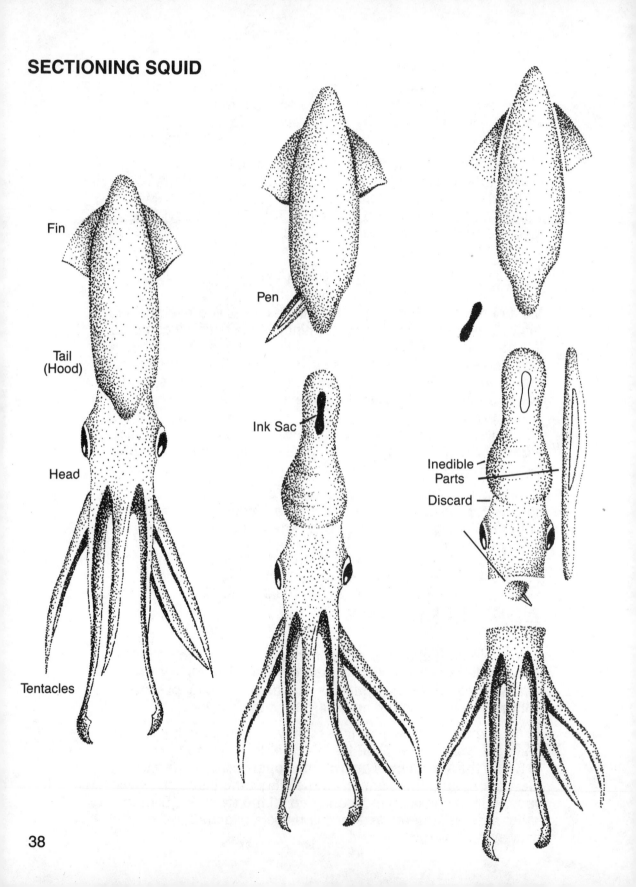

Fin

Tail
(Hood)

Head

Tentacles

Pen

Ink Sac

Inedible
Parts

Discard

CLEANING SQUID AND OCTOPUS

Often looked upon as escapees from a science fiction movie, squid and octopus have been shunned as food here in the United States for decades. Yet on the other side of the Atlantic, these same creatures are considered delicacies. Only recently have American seafood enthusiasts acquired a taste for these odd-shaped denizens of the deep.

SQUID—Almost all of the squid's surface area is edible: hood (tail), fins and yes, the tentacles! Also edible is the liquid found in the squid's ink sac, a small pouch located in the internal section of the hood and attached to the viscera. Inedible are the viscera, the head and eyes, the cellophane-like pen, and the beak and its surrounding tissue. These must be removed before cooking.

First soak the squid in cold water, then peel off the thin layer of skin. The tentacle suckers of large squid (longer than 8 inches) may be sharp and should be scraped off with a knife. Fold back the rim of the hood to locate the top of the cellophane-like pen. Grasp the pen by its tip, draw it out, and discard it. Grasp the squid firmly by the head and tentacles in one hand, and with the other hand pull the tail section away to separate. The viscera and ink sac should come away attached to the head and tentacles. The ink sac is often used to flavor or color a special dish and may be peeled away from the viscera and saved. Squeeze out any soft material from the hood and rinse out the hood thoroughly. The hood may be left whole for stuffing or cut into rings of about an inch wide. To prevent the rings from collapsing during cooking, turn them inside-out.

Remove and discard the head, eyes, and attached viscera by cutting through the squid at a point just below the eyes between the eyes and the tentacles. Locate and discard the squid's beak— it may have been cut away with the head and eyes or it may still be in the center core of the tentacles. To remove, push your finger through the underside of the tentacles' center core until the beak and its surrounding tissue pop out.

OCTOPUS—The skin of an octopus is not as easy to remove as that of a squid. To remove the skin of an octopus, rub the flesh with salt then peel the skin off with your fingers. Once skinned, soak the octopus in cold water for about ten minutes to wash off the salt.

Using heavy shears, cut off the tentacles at a point just below the eyes. Locate and discard the beak in the same manner as with squid. Turn the pouch inside out and pierce the membrane holding the viscera. Remove the viscera and the eyes. The ink sac in an octopus is covered with several membranes. To release it, carefully cut through the membrane and lift out the ink sac. Discard the viscera and eyes. Larger octopi may need tenderizing. To do so, pound the outside of the pouch with a wooden mallet, then turn the pouch inside-out and pound again.

To extract the dark black to brownish liquid from a squid's or octopus' ink sac, place the sacs in a fine sieve and with the back of a spoon mash the sacs to extract the ink.

CLEANING CONCH

To remove edible meat from a conch you must first sever the crown muscle which attaches the meat to the shell. Hold the conch crown side up and strike the shell about an inch below the crown with a hammer to make a hole large enough to admit the blade of a small knife. Insert the knife into the hole and direct it toward the crown. Move the knife around to sever the muscle. Grasp the ''foot'' which protrudes from the shell opening (not the hole you made) and pull out the meat. Cut away the soft material (the eyes and viscera) and trim off any hard areas of meat. Locate the intestinal vein which runs the length of the conch and cut it away. Peel off and discard the skin. To tenderize, pound the flesh on both sides with a wooden mallet until flat.

FREEZING EXCESS FISH

Quite often your day's catch outweighs your immediate needs. To preserve your surplus catch for future use after it has been cleaned it must be properly frozen. The first order of business is to determine how much fish you will need for one day's use, whether it be two steaks for you and your spouse or several pounds of fillet for a large family. Divide the fish into parcels, each representing one day's use. Wrap each unit of fish, steak, or fillet individually then wrap them together to form a parcel. Never wrap in one parcel more than you intend using at one time. And when one meal requires a large amount of fish, divide that amount into two or three smaller parcels.

Several criteria must be met when selecting wrapping material. It must be moisture proof; durable enough to resist tearing, cracking or puncturing; pliable enough to ensure a tight fit; and resistant to low temperatures. Aluminum foil, extra-strength plastic wrap (I use restaurant-size plastic cling wrap in 2000-foot rolls), and freezer paper meet such requirements.

Wrapping must be done in a way that prevents freezer burn, which occurs when moisture is allowed to escape due to improper packaging. This causes the fish's flesh to become dry and discolored. When wrapping, make sure the fish is completely covered and the wrapping material is pulled tight against the flesh to avoid air pockets where moisture can be lost.

The ideal temperature for freezing fish is 0 degrees Fahrenheit, although a range between 0 to 20 degrees is acceptable. When first placing wrapped fish into the freezer locate the coldest spot and arrange your parcels in that area. Avoid stacking at first to ensure even freezing. Once the parcels have been frozen solid, you may then rearrange them to your convenience.

There is no doubt that you can tell the difference between a blackfish and a flounder as each sails over the rail of a fishing boat. But once the fish have been cleaned, filleted or steaked, and wrapped for the freezer, it becomes a little difficult distinguishing one species from the other. Therefore it's a good idea to label each package of fish, indicating the species, the type of cut (fillet, steak, etc.) and, most importantly, the date. Although fish can be kept frozen indefinitely under ideal conditions, it's a good practice to use up frozen fish within a month's time.

Shellfish are best frozen in air-tight containers, the meat submerged in its own liquid or a brine solution. Shuck the clams or mussels, and remove crab and lobster meat from the shells and claws before freezing. To prepare a brine solution, dissolve one teaspoon of pure table salt for every pint of water. Chill the brine solution before adding it to the shellfish. Fill each container with shellfish meat and brine to within an inch to an inch and a half from the top. The shellfish should be completely covered by the brine solution. Cover tightly and freeze.

Once frozen solid, the block of frozen shellfish may be popped out of its container and wrapped tightly in foil or plastic wrap.

To defrost fish, remove the parcels from the freezer about 24 hours before using and place them on a plate in the bottom shelf of the refrigerator. In a pinch, you can speed up defrosting by submerging the frozen fish in cold water. As a final note, never defrost fish at room temperature, and never refreeze fish.

CHAPTER 3

A BASIC BEGINNING

by
AGLIANO

Sal

COOKING·WITH
Sal

3

A BASIC BEGINNING

The key to creating memorable seafood dishes lies in one basic rule: DON'T OVERCOOK! This applies especially when frying, baking, or broiling, and is less critical (although slightly) when poaching, stewing, or steaming.

Fish may be cooked by the same methods used for meats and poultry. However, the flesh of many warm-blooded creatures requires prolonged cooking to ensure tenderness and the destruction of harmful bacteria. Fish flesh, on the other hand, is naturally delicate and needs only a minimum of cooking time to ensure it's done, yet retains full flavor and succulence. Overcooking, in most cases, rapidly destroys flavor and texture as the fish becomes dry and tasteless.

The rule of thumb when cooking fish is to allow from 7 to 10 minutes of cooking time at moderate heat for every inch of fish at its thickest part. To test for doneness, pierce the flesh at the thickest point with a fork. If the meat is milky white and just beginning to flake, it's done! Once the flesh flakes easily, the fish has been overcooked.

Each chapter illustrates one mode of cooking as a preliminary introduction to seafood cuisine. Nothing fancy, nothing elaborate, nothing difficult—just a basic beginning!

BOILING

Because they're delicate, fish should never be put through the torture of rapid boiling. This only serves to break the meat apart as the agitated liquid rages uncontrollably. The only time to boil fish is when extracting flavors to prepare a stock for soups, stew, and sauces. Then, the liquid is used and the fish is discarded. And rather than sacrificing choice cuts such as fillets or steaks to make stock, use the scraps (heads, tails, fins, bones, and skin) to produce an exceptionally flavorful broth. The entrails and gills are inedible and should never be used in cooking.

To prepare a quart of fish stock, combine two quarts of cold water and two pounds of fish scraps in a kettle. Bring to a quick boil and continue to cook over high heat until the liquid is reduced by half. As scum rises to the surface, skim it off with a slotted spoon until no more rises. When done, remove the stock from the heat and allow to cool. Strain the cooled liquid through several layers of fine cheesecloth. Discard scraps.

POACHING

This is a method of gently simmering fish in a liquid such as water, fish stock, chicken broth, vegetable broth, wine, beer, milk—the choices are limited only by imagination and taste.

For fillets and pan-sized fish, a shallow pan filled with just enough liquid to rise an inch over the fish is best. For larger fish, you may need to use a fish poacher. This is an oblong pan, equipped with a rack and attached handles for easy removal of the cooked fish.

Poaching is not boiling, so the liquid should never progress beyond the simmering stage. Once the liquid is allowed to boil, flesh is likely to be torn from the fish.

POACHED
FLOUNDER FILLETS

Serves 4-6

2 lbs. flounder fillets
1 quart cold water
½ cup milk

1 lemon
1 tablespoon salt

In a shallow pan, combine water, milk, and salt. Cut the lemon into thin slices, pick out the seeds, and add the slices to the pan. Heat until the liquid begins to tremble. Gently slip in the fillets and simmer gently for about 5 minutes or until fillets pass the test for doneness.

With a slotted spatula, carefully remove the fillets, drain, and arrange on a platter. Top with a creamy sauce (Bechamel, Hollandaise, etc.—see chapter 15) and garnish with parsley sprigs and fresh lemon wedges.

POACHED
WHOLE WHITING

Serves 4-6

2 whiting (about 1 lb. each)
1 quart cold water

1 cup flat beer
1 teaspoon salt

Gut the whiting and remove their gills, leaving the heads and tails intact. Wrap each whiting in double-thickness cheesecloth leaving about three inches of extra cheesecloth on each end. Tie each end into a knot securing the fish.

Combine water, beer, and salt in a shallow pan. Heat to simmering. Lower the wrapped fish into the liquid. Cover the fish completely with poaching liquid, yet leave the knotted ends exposed for easy removal.

Cover the pan and simmer for 10 minutes. Gently remove the fish by grasping the knotted ends with pot holders. Carefully untie the knots and unwrap the fish onto a platter. Top with some of the pan liquid.

POACHED
CODFISH STEAKS
Serves 2

**2 codfish steaks
(4 to 6 ounces each)
2 quarts chicken stock
1 small onion, thinly sliced**

**1 carrot, cut into matchsticks
1 celery rib, diced
salt to taste**

Combine chicken stock, onion, carrot, celery, and salt in a shallow pan. Simmer over a low flame for about 15 minutes or until the vegetables are tender. Add fish steaks and simmer 10 to 15 minutes more or until steaks pass the test for doneness. Carefully remove the steaks and arrange on a platter. Top with broth and vegetables.

POACHED
WHOLE WEAKFISH
Serves 4-6

**1 weakfish
(about 2½ pounds)
1½ quarts cold water**

**1/2 cup white wine
1 onion, thinly sliced
1 teaspoon salt**

Combine water, wine, onion, and salt in a fish poacher large enough to hold the weakfish. Heat to simmering. Gut the weakfish and remove the gills, leaving the head and tail intact. Set the fish on the poaching rack and lower it into the liquid. Cover and poach for about 20 minutes or until a skewer inserted into the fish's thickest part passes through with little difficulty. Check often to make sure liquid doesn't boil. Lower flame if necessary or slide vessel off the burner for a moment.

When the fish is done, carefully raise the rack and slide the weakfish onto a platter. Serve whole or divided into portions.

To portion, carefully peel off the upper skin. Make a deep slash down the middle of the fish from head to tail. Make another slash across the fish from dorsal to ventral. Using a spatula, carefully lift out each section of meat. When each section is removed, lift the tail forward to remove it and the skeletal frame up to the head. Snip off the bone at the head. Divide the lower section of fish into portions. Slide the spatula between each portion and the underskin to remove.

STEAMING

Much like poaching, steaming uses moist heat to cook. But rather than being immersed in liquid, a fish is suspended above the boiling liquid and cooked by the rising steam. There are a multitude of devices used for steaming fish from a multi-chambered bamboo steamer common in Oriental cooking to a kettle fitted with a rack or basket. I prefer to use a large kettle equipped with a perforated insert which fits snugly over the kettle.

When using a bamboo steamer, each fish is placed on a plate deep enough to hold half a cup of liquid (usually a sauce) and wide enough to fit snugly in the steaming chamber. Whole fish are best slashed three or four times on both sides to accept the flavors of a light sauce generally poured over the fish before cooking. When using a rack, basket, or perforated insert, the fish may be placed on a plate or directly onto the steaming chamber bottom. With direct contact, the steaming chamber should be oiled lightly to prevent sticking.

Fill the bottom chamber with enough liquid (same choices as for poaching) to reach just below the upper section of the steamer. Cover and bring liquid to a boil. When the kettle is full of steam, place the fish into the upper chamber, cover and cook until done.

STEAMED TINKERS

**2 small mackerel
  (about 1/2 lb. each)
1 small onion, thinly sliced**

**2 cloves garlic, crushed
juice of half a lemon
salt and pepper to taste**

Gut the mackerel and remove their gills, leaving the heads and tails intact. Slash, then rub, the fish several times on both sides. Then rub the fish inside and out with salt, pepper, and garlic.

Allow the steaming vessel to fill with steam. Oil the upper chamber and add the fish. Pour lemon juice over the fish and spread the onion slices over and around the fish. Cover and steam for about 10 minutes or until fish pass the test for doneness.

STEAMED FLOUNDER FILLETS

Serves 2

4 flounder fillets
  (about 2 ounces each)
1 tablespoon butter, softened

2 cloves garlic, crushed
salt and pepper to taste
dashes of nutmeg

Allow the steaming vessel to fill with steam. Slide a heatproof plate into the upper chamber of the steamer and arrange the fillets on the plate. Mix the butter, garlic, salt, pepper, and nutmeg; brush mixture over the fillets. Cover and steam fillets for about 5 minutes or until done by testing.

STEAMED WEAKFISH STEAKS

Serves 4-6

2 weakfish steaks
  (4-6 ounces each)
juice of one lemon

dill weed
salt and pepper to taste

Allow the steaming vessel to fill with steam. Rub salt, pepper, and dill weed into the steaks on both sides. Oil the upper chamber of the steamer and put in the steaks. Dribble lemon juice over steaks, cover and steam for about 10 minutes or until done by testing.

STEWING

When is a seafood dish a stew and when is it soup? The answer lies more in attitude than in preparation and ingredients. If you approach the dish with spoon in hand and eagerly scoop up fish, vegetable, and broth in equal amounts, you are thinking soup! If you pierce each chunk of fish or vegetable separately, swirl it briefly in the broth and savor each morsel independently, you are thinking stew!

Basically, a stew is prepared with bite-size chunks of fish and vegetables, simmered in just enough liquid to support the ingredients. By contrast, a soup's ingredients are usually cut into smaller pieces and cooked in more liquid.

BASIC FISH STEW   Serves 4-6

2 lbs. mixed fish fillet
    (cod, flounder, etc.)
1 small onion, diced
2 cloves garlic, crushed
3 potatoes, cut into eighths
1 carrot, cut into
    1-inch pieces
1 celery rib,
    cut into 1/2-inch pieces
1 teaspoon thyme
salt and pepper to taste
1 tablespoon butter
4 cups water

Melt the butter in a 4-quart kettle. Add onions and garlic; saute briefly, until onions are limp. Add water, potatoes, carrot, celery, and thyme. Simmer for about 20 minutes or until vegetables are slightly tender. Cut fillets into chunks and add to the kettle. Simmer for about 15 minutes or until flesh begins to flake. Serve hot.

BRAISING

Although similar preparations are used in both braising and stewing, the results are quite different. When braising, the vegetables are used for flavoring. After cooking, they are either discarded or used to prepare a sauce for the fish.

BRAISED PORGIES
Serves 4

4 porgies
  (about 1/2 lb. each)
2 tablespoons butter
1 cup minced onions
1 cup minced carrots
1 cup minced celery
1 bell pepper, minced

2 cloves garlic, crushed
1 teaspoon chopped
  fresh parsley
1 teaspoon thyme
1 cup white wine
fish stock (about 2 cups)
salt and pepper to taste

Pan dress the porgies (with or without tails) and set aside in the refrigerator. Melt butter in a skillet. Add onions, carrots, celery, bell pepper, and garlic. Saute vegetables until lightly browned.

Transfer sauteed vegetables to a 4-quart kettle. Stir in the parsley and thyme and arrange the porgies over the vegetables. Add the wine, salt, and pepper, then pour in enough fish stock to cover fish. Cover the kettle and simmer for about 15 minutes or until fish test done when pierced with a fork.

Transfer fish to a platter and keep warm. Drain and puree vegetables in a food processor. Mix pureed vegetables with two tablespoons Lemon Roux (see chapter 15) and enough pan liquid to make a smooth sauce. Pour over fish.

PAN FRYING

When is a fish no longer considered pan-size? Simple: when it reaches a length where it no longer fits in a frypan. The most likely candidates for pan frying are: porgies, snapper blues, butterfish, white perch, lafayettes, tommy cod and tinker mackerel. Fillets may also be pan fried although a watchful eye is recommended to prevent overcooking. Fillets and skinned fish should be coated with a dry, starchy substance such as flour, corn starch or crumbs before frying to prevent the flesh from drying. A hot skillet and a thin layer of oil are the prerequisites for pan frying. Butter may be used, but it should be mixed with some oil to prevent burning. A perfectly done fish is pan fried in moments as the intense heat seals the outer skin while leaving the interior moist. But a moment too long in the frypan and the fish is overcooked beyond repair.

PAN FRIED FLOUNDER FILLETS

Serves 2-4

4 flounder fillets
flour
salt and pepper to taste

1/2 cup softened butter
1/4 cup oil

Sift flour, salt, and pepper onto a plate. Dust fillets on both sides with flour mix. Heat a skillet and add butter. When the butter just begins to foam, stir in the oil until hot. Slip in the fillets and fry quickly on both sides until golden brown.

Arrange the fish on a platter. Pour the pan liquid through a strainer and over the fish. Garnish with parsley sprigs and lemon wedges.

PAN FRIED SNAPPERS Serves 4-6

6-10 snappers
** (about 6 inches long)**
corn meal

garlic powder
oil

Pan dress the snappers and rub with garlic powder. Roll the snappers in corn meal until thoroughly coated. Heat a skillet and add about half an inch of oil. When the oil heats, slip in the snappers one at a time and fry on both sides until golden brown.

STIR FRYING (SAUTEING)

Orientals call it stir frying; Western Civilization seems content with the term sauteing. In either instance, it is a quick and efficient method to cook fish. A minimum of oil is used to fry the fish over high heat for a short period of time. The ingredients which have been cut into bite-size pieces are constantly stirred and turned until done.

STIR FRIED FISH

Serves 4-6

2 lbs. fillet
   (flounder, sea bass, etc.)
1 onion, minced
2 scallions, cut into strips
2 whole cloves garlic

1 egg white, lightly beaten
2 tablespoons corn starch
salt and pepper to taste
oil

Cut the fillets into cubes or strips and combine in a bowl with egg white, corn starch, salt and pepper. Toss lightly.

Heat a skillet or wok and add enough oil to coat the pan. When the oil is hot, put in the garlic and fry until brown. Remove garlic and discard. Add onion and scallions and stir fry until limp. Add fish pieces and stir fry until fish is lightly browned. Remove fish and vegetables with a slotted spoon, allowing the oil to drain. Garnish with lemon wedges.

DEEP FRYING

Light dusting is sufficient when pan frying or stir frying, but when deep frying, fish must be thoroughly coated to seal in flavor and maintain succulence. Although you are allowed some leeway in cooking time, too long on the fire and the fish are destroyed!

Deep fried fish are usually coated first in beaten egg, then once again in a dry, starchy substance such as flour or bread crumbs. The oil must reach a temperature of at least 350 degrees before cooking—375 is ideal. The coated fish are slipped into the hot oil (one at a time to prevent sticking) then cooked until golden brown. Remove the fish from the oil with a slotted spoon, pausing momentarily over the oil to drain. The fish are then placed on paper towels for additional draining. You may also use a frying basket which is lifted out of the oil once the fish are cooked.

DEEP FRIED FISH (FLOURED)

Serves 4-6

2 lbs. fish fillets　　　　**flour**
　(flounder, cod, etc.)　**oil**
2 eggs, slightly beaten

Cut the fillets into chunks about 1 inch long. Dip each fish piece into beaten egg, then roll in flour until well coated. Heat a deep frying kettle and fill it halfway with oil. Heat the oil until the temperature reaches at least 350 degrees (use a thermometer designed for deep fryers or test by dropping a bread cube into the oil; if the bread browns in moments, the oil is hot).

Carefully lower the floured fish into the hot oil and fry on both sides until golden brown. Drain on paper towels.

DEEP FRIED FISH (BREADED)

Serves 4-6

**2 lbs. fish fillets
(flounder, cod, etc.)
flour
2 eggs, slightly beaten**

**2 cups dry crumbs
(see note below)
oil**

Cut the fillets into chunks and dust each piece with flour. Dip the floured fish into beaten egg and roll in crumbs until well coated. Heat oil as described in the last recipe and fry fish until golden brown. Drain on paper towels. NOTE: the crumbs may be bread crumbs, cracker meal, matzo meal or crushed corn flakes.

DEEP FRIED FISH (BATTER)

Serves 4-6

**2 lbs. fish fillets
(flounder, cod, etc.)
1 cup flour
1 tablespoon light oil**

**1 egg, slightly beaten
1 cup warm beer
oil for deep frying**

In a mixing bowl, combine the beaten egg, light oil and beer. Sift the flour into the bowl and mix until batter is free of lumps. Set aside for about an hour—this allows the flour to absorb the liquid which improves the clinging power of the batter.

Cut the fillets into chunks. Heat the oil as described in previous recipes. Stab each chunk of fish with a fork and dip into the batter. Twirl the fish to coat evenly and lift and hold briefly over the batter to allow the excess to drip off. With another fork, slide the coated fish into the hot oil. Cook fish until golden brown. Drain on paper towels.

BAKING

Baking is one of the least complicated methods of cooking fish, yet if the fish are unattended, disaster is eminent! Baking is a dry form of cooking and inasmuch as fish have little internal moisture to keep their flesh from drying out, cooking time must be precise. Again, I must stress the rule mentioned earlier in this chapter; it certainly applies when baking fish!

Measure the fish at its thickest part and bake from 7 to 10 minutes for every inch of thickness. Check often for doneness by piercing the flesh at its thickest point.

Basting offers additional protection against drying. The liquids used for basting are oil, butter, lemon juice, fish stock, vegetable broth, or a combination of ingredients. Basting liquid may be flavored with a variety of spices. Fish may also be baked partially submerged in liquid.

Another precaution is wrapping the fish in foil or, as the Greeks have done for centuries, grape leaves. This traps the moisture and reduces the risk of the fish drying out. Lettuce leaves may also be used to exude and retain moisture.

Fish dressed in any form (whole, steaked, filleted) may be baked with satisfactory results. Fish may be stuffed and fillets may be rolled and baked, but thicknesses should be measured after stuffing or rolling.

BAKED BLUEFISH   Serves 6-8

**1 bluefish
 (about 5 pounds)
salt and pepper to taste**

**garlic powder
white wine (about a cup)
lemon juice**

Pan dress the bluefish, then rub salt and pepper inside and out. Stir together the wine and lemon juice and brush lightly over the bluefish. Set the fish on a rack in a roasting pan and sprinkle with garlic powder. Preheat the oven to 425 degrees and bake the bluefish for 7 to 10 minutes for every inch of thickness. Baste frequently. Check for doneness by piercing a skewer into the fish's thickest part. If a little resistance is met, the fish is done.

BAKED CODFISH STEAKS

Serves 2-4

**2 codfish steaks
(4-6 ounces each)**

**salt and pepper to taste
juice of one lemon**

Brush the codfish steaks on both sides with lemon juice, then sprinkle with salt and pepper. Place the steaks into a baking pan and fill the pan with water until steaks are partially submerged. Bake in a preheated oven set at 425 degrees 7 to 10 minutes for every inch of thickness.

BAKED FLUKE FILLETS

Serves 4-6

**1 fluke (about 2½ lbs.)
salt and pepper to taste
1 lemon
1 teaspoon minced garlic**

**1 teaspoon finely
chopped parsley
1 tablespoon butter**

Scale and fillet the fluke leaving the skins on. Place the fillets, skin-side-down, in baking pan. Sprinkle with salt and pepper. Top with garlic and parsley and set a dab of butter in the center of each fillet. Cut the lemon into paper-thin slices and arrange over the fillets. Dribble a little water into the pan—just enough to cover the bottom.

Bake in a preheated oven set at 425 degrees for 7 to 10 minutes for every inch of thickness. Test for doneness.

BROILING

When most folks think of cooking fish, broiling inevitably comes to mind. It is another form of dry cooking which requires additional liquid to prevent drying. The source of heat is directly above with no barrier between the flame and the fish. Cooking is swift, so constant attention is necessary to achieve perfection.

To broil fish, preheat the broiler for about 15 minutes. Brush the fish with basting liquid (oil, butter, lemon juice, fish stock) and arrange the fish on a broiling rack. For cuts of fish one inch thick, position the rack 4 to 6 inches below the flame. For larger cuts, position the rack one inch lower for every half inch of thickness. Broil the fish for 7 to 10 minutes for every inch of thickness. Check often, if premature browning occurs, reposition the fish one notch lower. Turn the fish once halfway through cooking. Whole fish may be broiled, but for more uniform cooking it is best to first split the fish. Fillets and steaks are exceptional choices for broiling.

BROILED PORGIES   Serves 2-4

**2 porgies
  (about 1 lb. each)
1/4 cup oil
juice of one lemon
salt and pepper to taste**

**2 cloves garlic, crushed
1 teaspoon finely
  chopped parsley
1/2 teaspoon paprika**

Scale and pan dress the porgies, then set aside. Combine oil, lemon juice, salt, pepper, garlic, parsley and paprika in a bowl. Stir until well blended. Place the porgies into the marinade and set aside in the refrigerator for about one hour.

Preheat the broiler for about 15 minutes. Place the porgies on a broiling rack and brush on additional marinade. Broil for 7 to 10 minutes for every inch of thickness, turning the fish once halfway through cooking. Baste several times during cooking.

BROILED CODFISH STEAKS

Serves 2-4

2 codfish steaks
  (4-6 ounces each)
1/4 cup oil

juice of one lemon
salt and pepper to taste
1/2 teaspoon dill

Prepare a marinade by mixing oil, lemon juice, salt, pepper and dill. Set the steaks in a shallow dish and pour on marinade. Refrigerate for about one hour.

Preheat the broiler and place the marinated codfish steaks on a broiling rack. Brush the steaks with additional marinade. Broil for 7 to 10 minutes for every inch of thickness, turning the steaks once halfway through cooking.

BROILED BLUEFISH FILLETS

Serves 4-6

1 bluefish
  (about 2 pounds)
1/4 cup oil
1/2 cup white wine

2 cloves garlic, crushed
dash of cayenne pepper/
  salt to taste

Scale and fillet the bluefish leaving the skins on. Place the fillets in a shallow pan and pour a marinade of oil, wine, garlic, salt, pepper and enough water to cover fish. Refrigerate for about one hour.

Preheat the oven and place the bluefish fillets, skin-side-down, onto a broiling rack. Brush the fillets with additional marinade and broil 7 to 10 minutes for every inch of thickness; baste several times during cooking. Cook only on one side.

BARBECUING

Barbecuing is nothing more than outdoor broiling with an additional element—smoke! Nothing beats the smoky flavor of a freshly caught fish cooked on an outdoor grill.

The heat source when barbecuing is from below rather than above as when broiling in an oven. The timing formula prescribed for broiling indoors can only be a rough guideline when barbecuing in the open. The heat of your outdoor grill is constantly affected by temperature, wind and humidity. To compensate, it is best to test often for doneness when cooking fish on an outdoor grill.

Whole fish, fillets, or steaks that can be broiled indoors may also be barbecued with satisfactory results. Hamburgers and hot dogs may do well on the barbecue's permanent grill, but when cooking fish it is best to invest a few bucks, in a doublesided, hinged barbecuing basket. This gadget allows you to turn the fish with little concern about your meal breaking apart. To prevent sticking, the basket should be brushed with oil before enclosing the fish.

Allow the coals to burn for at least half an hour before cooking the fish. Spread the coals flat for cooking fish of even thickness and bank the coals under the thickest parts of fish of uneven thickness. Turn the fish once halfway through cooking and test often for doneness.

WHOLE WEAKFISH BARBECUE

Serves 6-8

1 weakfish
  (about 3 pounds)
1 cup melted butter

salt and pepper to taste
garlic powder
juice of one lemon

Scale, gut, and remove the gills from the weakfish, leaving the head and tail intact. Slash the fish slightly on both sides along the body. Sprinkle salt, pepper and garlic powder over the fish, inside and out. Mix together the melted butter and lemon juice. Brush butter/lemon mixture lightly over the fish.

Oil the barbecuing basket and lock in the fish. Place over hot coals about 3 inches away. Barbecue on one side until skewer inserted into the cooked side just below the gill plate meets little resistance. Turn the basket over and cook the weakfish on the other side, testing for doneness in the same manner. Baste several times during cooking with butter/lemon mixture.

BARBECUED BLUEFISH STEAKS

Serves 2-4

2 bluefish steaks
  (4-6 ounces each)
1 cup oil
1 teaspoon brown sugar

1/4 cup ketchup
2 tablespoons vinegar
salt and pepper to taste

Mix the oil, brown sugar, ketchup, vinegar, salt and pepper. Brush mixture over both sides of the steaks. Lock the steaks in a barbecuing basket and set 3 inches over the hot coals. Cook on both sides until done by testing; baste frequently.

MICROWAVE COOKING

For the busy fisherman who wants to spend as little time in the kitchen as possible, microwave cooking may be the answer. Microwaves are high frequency radio waves which cause liquids to vibrate at such high speeds the resulting friction creates sufficient heat to cook. Microwave cooking is about four times faster than conventional cooking methods— therefore the timing formula mentioned throughout this chapter must be adjusted to compensate for this space age cooking technique.

To gauge fish for microwave cooking, allow 1 to 3 minutes of cooking time for every inch of thickness. When in doubt, it is best to under cook the fish, test it for doneness, then return it to the microwave oven for further cooking, if necessary. Once the fish is overcooked, there is nothing you can do to save the meal.

Microwaves act in three ways depending on which material is introduced into the oven. Metal objects reflect microwaves. Food contained in a metal utensil will not receive the microwaves or at best only a minimum of waves needed to cook sufficiently. Even containers with metal bands or handles will drastically affect the outcome of your cooking.

Microwaves pass through materials such as glass, ceramic, paper, and certain plastics. Many containers of such materials are specifically designed for microwave use.

Microwaves are absorbed by materials that are moist—all foods contain enough moisture for microwave absorption. From that point a chain reaction occurs as the liquid molecules begin to vibrate and cooking commences by both friction and conduction.

FLOUNDER IN WINE SAUCE
Serves 2-4

1 lb. flounder fillet   **1 teaspoon butter**
1/3 cup dry white wine   **salt and pepper to taste**

Select a shallow pan specifically designed for microwave cooking. Combine the wine, butter, salt, and pepper in the pan. Place the fillets, side by side in the pan of liquid. Cover and place into the microwave. Set the heat control prescribed in your microwave manual for fish (usually it's the highest setting). Cook for 1 to 3 minutes for every inch of thickness. Remove fish from the microwave and test for doneness.

CHAPTER 4

MASTERPIECES OF FRENCH COOKING

by
AGLIANO

Sal

4

MASTERPIECES OF FRENCH COOKING

When I was fresh out of high school, I worked side by side with a master French chef. No, I wasn't lucky enough to have gained employment in a fancy French restaurant—actually I was a counterman and the French chef (his name was Terry, but we called him Frenchie) was a short order cook; both of us were rattling pots and pans in a fast food joint in lower Manhattan.

There was nothing unusual about my working in such an establishment—I was inexperienced. But why was a chef of Frenchie's credentials slinging hash, so to speak, in a diner?

Well, Frenchie had a habit of pouring more wine into his goblet than into coq au vin, and as a result he had earned an unfavorable reputation throughout some of the finer restaurants in New York. By the time he had curbed his thirst for the grape, he had already slipped to the bottom of the rung of the culinary ladder.

Frenchie eventually regained his former status, but before doing so, he enriched my life along with expanding my appreciation for fine cooking. From Frenchie I learned techniques as basic as flipping eggs in a frypan and as elaborate as deglazing a pan with wine in preparation for an exquisite French sauce.

French chefs, like my old friend, take cooking seriously, placing as much emphasis on the artistic as well as the culinary aspects of cooking. Some say, you need only look at a French dish and you could almost taste it. A meticulously and lovingly prepared french dish is more than just another meal—it is a masterpiece!

BOUILLABAISSE

The Mona Lisa of French Cooking, this classic fish stew was originally prepared with whatever fish were left over after a day's haul. What the fisherman couldn't sell at the market they tossed into the pot for Bouillabaisse!

3 lbs. mixed fish fillets (include sea robins and conger eels)

1 quart fresh clams and/or mussels

4 lbs. fish scraps (heads, tails, skin, and bones)

4 quarts water

1 cup dry white wine

1/2 cup olive oil

4-8 cloves garlic, crushed

2 onions, sliced thinly

1 cup chopped leeks

1 cup chopped fennel (bulb, stalk, and leaves)

1/2 cup chopped celery

4-6 large ripe tomatoes

1 teaspoon crushed red hot pepper

pinch of saffron

peel of one whole orange

2 bay leaves

1 teaspoon thyme

1 teaspoon rosemary

salt and pepper to taste

1/4 cup chopped fresh parsley

SAUCE ROUILLE (see chapter 15)

Combine the water, wine, fish scraps, an orange peel in a large kettle and boil until liquid is reduced by half. Strain the liquid and discard the scraps and orange peel. Return the stock to the kettle and simmer gently.

Heat a large frypan, then add the olive oil. When the oil becomes hot, add the garlic, onions, leeks, fennel and celery; saute briefly. Core and peel the tomatoes, cut them into chunks and add to the frypan. Cook for about ten minutes, stirring continuously. Remove the frypan from the heat and stir in the red pepper and saffron. Transfer the frypan ingredients to kettle. Prepare a bouquet garni by tying the bay leaves, thyme, and rosemary in a wad of cheesecloth. Drop the bouquet garni into the kettle and simmer for 20 minutes.

Meanwhile, scrub the shellfish and cut the fillet into chunks. After the stock has cooked for 20 minutes, add the shellfish and fillet along with salt and pepper; simmer for 20 minutes.

When done, remove and discard the bouquet garni. Stir parsley and about a cup of SAUCE ROUILLE into the fish stew. Place two or three slices of toasted french bread into deep bowls and ladle the fish stew over the bread. Serve hot!

FISH QUENELLES

Serves 4-6

These tasty little dumplings are so light and fluffy you would almost expect them to float off the plate. But don't worry… they'll stay put for you to enjoy.

1 lb. fish fillet (cod, flounder, sea bass, etc.)
2 egg whites
1/4 cup heavy cream
1 teaspoon salt
1/4 teaspoon white pepper
2 tablespoons chopped fresh parsley

dash of nutmeg
COURT BOUILLON (see chapter 15)
BECHAMEL SAUCE (see chapter 15)

Grind the fillet in a food processor. Add egg whites, cream, salt, pepper, and nutmeg; whip until light and fluffy. Transfer mix to a bowl, fold in parsley, cover and refrigerate for about one hour.

In a large kettle, heat 3 quarts of COURT BOUILLON. With a large spoon, scoop up mounds of fish mixture and slide them into the hot broth one at a time. Cover and simmer for 15 minutes.

Carefully remove the cooked quenelles from the broth with a slotted spoon, drain over the kettle and arrange on a platter. Spoon hot BECHAMEL SAUCE over the quenelles. Serve hot!

CRAB QUENELLES

Serves 4-6

Substitute 1 pound of cooked crabmeat for the fish fillets in the previous recipe.

FANCY QUENELLES

Serves 4-6

Instead of all fish or all crab, mix 1/2 pound of fish, 1/2 pound of cooked crab, and 1/2 cup coarsley chopped cooked baby shrimp. Prepare in the same manner as the previous recipes.

BROILED QUENELLES   Serves 4-6

12 fish, crab or   **1 tablespoon butter**
   fancy quenelles
2 cups BECHAMEL SAUCE
   (see chapter 15)

Prepare the quenelles as you would in the previous recipes, drain and set aside. Melt the butter in a shallow baking pan large enough to hold the 12 quenelles. Arrange the quenelles, side by side, in the baking pan. Pour the BECHAMEL SAUCE over the quenelles.

Preheat the broiler, then slide the pan of quenelles about 4 inches below the flame. Broil for about 10 minutes or until quenelles are lightly browned.

CRAB/ASPARAGUS QUICHE

Serves 4-8

A quiche is a main dish custard pie baked in a flaky crust. You can serve it hot from the oven (although it may be a little loose), cold the next day, or as I prefer it, at room temperature.

CRUST

1½ cups flour   ice water
1/4 pound butter or
   margarine (1 stick)

Crumble the butter in a medium sized mixing bowl. Add the flour, then with the tines of a fork blend the flour into the butter until they resemble coarse meal.

While mixing, add one teaspoon of ice water at a time until the dough holds together. Shape the dough into a ball, wrap in waxed paper and refrigerate.

After about 15 minutes, roll the dough out on a well-floured surface to a thickness of about 1/4 inch. Fit the rolled dough into a 9-inch pie or quiche pan and press into place. Trim the excess dough from around the rim of the pan. With a fork, prick the dough several times at the bottom of the pan and flute the rim to decorate. Bake in a preheated oven set at 400 degrees for about 15 minutes.

FILLING

1 cup cooked crabmeat   1 cup heavy cream
1/2 pound cooked asparagus   1 cup milk
   tips, well drained   salt and white pepper to taste
4 eggs, beaten

Combine the crabmeat, eggs, cream, milk, salt and pepper in a large bowl. Mix just until blended. Pour mixture into the baked crust. Arrange the asparagus tips over the top of the mixture in a circular pattern...be creative! Bake in a preheated oven set at 375 degrees for about half an hour or until a knife inserted into the center of the quiche comes out clean. Just before serving cut the quiche into wedges.

FLOUNDER QUICHE

Serves 4-8

1 9-inch pastry crust
   (see previous recipe)
1 lb. flounder fillet,
   cut into long strips
1 cup chopped roasted
   peppers, drained well

4 eggs, beaten
1 cup heavy cream
1 cup milk
salt and white pepper to taste

Bake the pastry crust as described in the previous recipe. In a large bowl, combine the chopped peppers, eggs, cream, milk, salt and pepper; mix just until blended. Pour half of the mixture into the baked crust. Arrange the flounder strips over the mixture in a circular pattern. Gently spoon the rest of the mixture over the fillets; smooth it out evenly. Bake in a preheated oven set at 375 degrees for about half an hour or until a knife inserted in the center of the quiche comes out clean. Serve in wedges.

CRAB AND CHEDDAR CHEESE SOUFFLE

Serves 4-6

1 cup cooked crabmeat
1/2 cup shredded
   cheddar cheese
2 tablespoons butter
2 tablespoons flour
1¼ cup hot milk

3 egg yolks
5 egg whites
2 tablespoons
   chopped chives
salt and white pepper to taste

In a saucepan, melt the butter over a low heat until it just begins to foam. Add the flour and stir vigorously until blended (I use a metal whisk). Remove from heat and pour in the hot milk while mixing. Continue mixing until smooth. Return to heat and cook while stirring until mixture has thickened to the consistency of a pudding. Remove from the heat and set aside. This is a thicker version of BECHAMEL SAUCE.

Beat the egg yolks in a bowl. Add the hot sauce one spoonful at a time, whisking until smooth after each addition. When half of the hot sauce has been incorporated into the egg, pour the rest of the sauce into the egg and whisk until smooth. Set aside a pinch of cheddar cheese to be used later as a topping. Put the remaining cheese into the sauce along with the crabmeat, salt, pepper, chives; stir until just blended.

In a clean, dry bowl, beat the egg whites with an electric mixer until stiff peaks form. Pour the stiffened egg whites over the sauce and with a rubber spatula gently lift the bottom of the mixture over the top several times. This method is called "folding" and must be done gently. Don't mix too thoroughly. When finished, you should have patches of yolk and white.

Gently pour the mixture into a well-greased souffle pan (any tall, rounded cooking vessel of about 4 quart capacity will do). The mixture should come to about three quarters from the top of the pan. Sprinkle on the remaining cheese and bake in a preheated oven set at 400 degrees for about half an hour or until the souffle has risen over the top of the pan and is golden brown.

A souffle is a delicate work of culinary art and should be served right from the oven. Wait too long and the souffle will collapse!

CRAB AND CHEESE OMELET WITH MUSHROOM SAUCE

1 cup cooked crabmeat
1/4 cup shredded swiss or
   cheddar cheese
6 eggs
salt and pepper to taste
1 cup BECHAMEL SAUCE
   (see chapter 15)

1/2 pound fresh mushrooms,
   chopped coarsely
1/4 cup minced onion
1/2 cup dry white wine
butter

Prepare the sauce first, then keep it warm while you fix the omelets. In a saucepan, melt a dab of butter then saute the mushrooms and onions until the onions are lightly browned. Add the BECHAMEL SAUCE and the wine, and simmer while mixing until sauce is smooth.

In a bowl, beat the eggs lightly. Add the crabmeat, cheese, salt and pepper; mix lightly. Using an omelet pan, a crepe pan, or a flat skillet, melt about 1 tablespoon of butter then pour 1/4 of the egg mixture into the pan. Tilt the pan in all directions to spread the mixture evenly. Cook over medium heat until the edges of the omelet become firm. Using a wide spatula, poke under the omelet to free it from the pan, then fold one half of the omelet over the other.

Continue to cook until firm. Slide the omelet off the pan and onto an individual plate; keep warm. Prepare three more omeletes using the remainder of the mixture. Reheat the mushroom sauce and pour over the omelet. Garnish with parsley sprigs. Serve hot!

FLOUNDER WITH FINE HERBS

This dish is traditionally prepared with sole fillets. But since true sole are rarely caught by fishermen of the North Atlantic, I've found our local flounder an ideal choice for this classic French dish.

2 lbs. fluke or flounder
fillets
FISH FUMET
(see chapter 15)
1/2 lb. butter,
cut into 1/2-inch chips

salt and pepper to taste
1 tablespoon chopped
fresh parsley
1 teaspoon chopped chives
1 teaspoon tarragon

Sprinkle the fillets on both sides with salt and pepper. Place a chip of butter in the center of each fillet, roll the fillets and secure with wooden toothpicks. Arrange the rolled fillets in the bottom of a shallow pan, sprinkle on the parsley, chives and tarragon, then add enough FISH FUMET to cover the fillets. Bring to just below a boil, remove from heat and set aside to continue cooking.

After about 15 minutes carefully remove the fillets, drain and set aside on a warm platter. Boil the liquid until it has been reduced to about 2 cups. Lower the flame to a simmer, then add the remaining butter chips, one at a time, stirring continuously. When the last chip of butter has been blended into the liquid, remove the pan from the heat. The sauce should be syrupy. Pour the sauce over the fillets. Serve hot!

SEA BASS WITH SHRIMP L'ORANGE

I've always found the subtle flavor of orange a welcome accompaniment to seafood. In this dish, the blending of orange peel and brandy adds a new dimension of seafood dining.

2 lbs. sea bass fillets
1 pint orange juice
1 pint water
1 cup BECHAMEL SAUCE
   (see chapter 15)
1 tablespoon orange juice
   concentrate

1 cup cooked baby shrimp
1 tablespoon minced
   orange peel
1 oz. (make it a shot)
   of brandy or cognac
1 teaspoon tarragon

In a small bowl, soak the orange peel in the brandy; set aside. Combine the orange juice and water in a shallow pan and simmer. When the liquid just begins to bubble, slip in the fillets and poach until fish test done. Remove the fillets from the pan, drain, and keep warm.

Heat the BECHAMEL SAUCE. Add the orange juice concentrate, shrimp, tarragon, orange peel and the brandy. Heat briefly while stirring until ingredients are well blended and the sauce is bubbly.

Pour the sauce over the fillets, garnish with sprigs of parsley and orange wedges. Serve hot!

BLUEFISH IN VERMOUTH

Serves 4-6

1 bluefish
  (about 2½ lbs.)
1 cup Vermouth
water
2 cloves garlic

salt and pepper to taste
1/4 lb. butter, cut into
  1/2 inch chips
1/2 cup heavy cream
dash of nutmeg

Scale and fillet the bluefish, leaving its skin on. Rub the garlic into the flesh of each fillet, then sprinkle with salt and pepper. Place the fillets, skin side down, in a shallow baking pan. Pour Vermouth into the pan and add just enough water to cover the fillets. Chill in refrigerator.

After an hour, drain the liquid and set it aside to be used later to prepare the sauce. Preheat the broiler and slip the bluefish about 4 inches below the flame. Broil the fillets until they test done. Transfer to a hot platter and keep warm.

Pour about two cups of the Vermouth mixture into a saucepan. Heat until the liquid begins to simmer. Add the butter, one chip at a time, to the liquid while stirring continuously until all the butter is used. Slowly pour in the heavy cream and stir briefly. Remove the sauce from the heat and stir in the nutmeg. Strain the sauce then pour it over the bluefish fillets. Garnish with sprigs of parsley. Serve hot!

SEATROUT ALMONDINE

Serves 4-6

Although it closely resembles freshwater trout, our local weakfish is actually a croaker. But we'll overlook that basic fact when preparing this dish originally intended for the freshwater species.

2 weakfish fillets
1 egg
1 cup milk
flour
butter

1/2 cup slivered almonds
juice of 1/2 a lemon
1/2 teaspoon tarragon
salt and pepper to taste

Beat the eggs in a bowl, then add the milk, salt and pepper; mix until blended. Pour about a cup of flour on a plate. Dip the fillets on both sides into the egg mixture, then dredge in flour.

Heat a frypan, then melt enough butter to fill the bottom of the pan. Saute the fillets on both sides until done by testing—add more butter as needed. Transfer the fillets to a warm platter.

Wipe the frypan, then add 2 tablespoons of butter. When the butter begins to foam, add the almonds and saute until lightly browned. Remove the pan from the heat; add the lemon juice and tarragon. Stir briefly. Pour the almonds and butter over the fillets. Serve hot!

TILEFISH ALMONDINE

Serves 4-6

I've never had the opportunity to nail a tilefish, but I've often savored its succulent flesh thanks to several fishing buddies who ventured offshore. I still haven't decided whether this deepwater fish tastes like lobster, blackfish or porgy.

**2 tilefish steaks
(about 6 ounces each)
1/2 cup milk
2 tablespoons butter**

**1/2 cup slivered almonds
1 teaspoon parsley
2 cloves garlic, sliced
salt and pepper to taste**

Melt the butter in a frypan, then saute the almonds and garlic until lightly browned. Place the tilefish steaks in a lightly oiled baking pan. Brush the steaks with milk and season with salt and pepper. Pour the almonds, garlic and butter over the steaks, sprinkle on parsley and bake in a preheated oven set at 425 degrees for about 15 minutes or until steaks test done.

CODFISH MEDALLION CHAMPIGNON

Serves 4-6

The simple procedure of trimming a fish steak into a medallion is explained in chapter two.

2 codfish medallions
  (about 4 ounces each)
1/2 lb. fresh mushrooms,
  coarsely chopped
1/2 cup minced onions
1/4 cup chopped leeks
2 cloves garlic, sliced

2 tablespoons butter
juice of 1/2 a lemon
1 cup BECHAMEL SAUCE
  (see chapter 15)
1/4 cup dry white wine
salt and pepper to taste

Season the medallions with salt and pepper and set aside. Heat a frypan and melt the butter. When the butter begins to foam, add the onions, leeks and garlic; saute briefly. Add the mushrooms and continue to saute until mushrooms are lightly browned. Remove the pan from the heat and add the lemon juice, stir briefly. Add the BECHAMEL SAUCE and the wine. Return to heat and cook briefly while stirring until ingredients are blended and the sauce has thickened.

Place the codfish medallions in a baking pan. Pour the mushroom sauce over and around the fish. Bake in a preheated oven set at 425 degrees for about 15 minutes or until fish test done. Serve hot!

RAIE AU BUERRE NOIR
(skate wings in black butter)   Serves 4

4 skate wings   **1 cup BEURRE NOIR**
1 small onion, minced   **(see chapter 15)**
1 bay leaf

Place the skate wings, onions, and bay leaf in a medium size saucepan. Pour in enough cold water to cover the wings, then simmer, covered for 20 minutes.

After 20 minutes, pick out and discard the bay leaf. Drain the onions and skate wings, then separate the wings from the onions. When the wings have cooled enough for handling, peel off the skin and trim away any hard spots along the edges.

Place the wings onto a warm platter, top with minced onions, then prepare a black butter sauce (BUERRE NOIR) as explained in chapter 15. Pour the hot sauce over the skate wings. Serve hot!

RAIE AU ESPINADE ET CREME

(skate wings with creamed spinach)   Serves 4

4 skate wings
1 lb. fresh or 10 oz.
  frozen chopped spinach
1 cup heavy cream (1/2 pint)

2 tablespoons butter
juice of 1/2 a lemon
salt and pepper to taste

Poach the skate wings in water for 20 minutes. Drain and skin. Cook the chopped spinach in salted water until barely tender. Drain and squeeze out any excess water.

In a frypan, melt the butter until it begins to foam. Add the spinach and saute briefly. Remove from the heat, stir in the heavy cream, lemon juice, salt and pepper. Arrange the wings on a platter, then top with creamed spinach. Serve hot!

CRAB MORNAY

Serves 4-6

2 cups cooked crabmeat
1 cup MORNAY SAUCE
  (see chapter 15)

French bread, thinly sliced
butter, slightly softened
chopped parsley

Combine the crabmeat and MORNAY SAUCE in a saucepan and heat over a low flame until sauce begins to bubble.

While the sauce is cooking, spread a thin smear of butter over the bread slices. Pop under the broiler and toast lightly.

Arrange the bread slices on a large platter. Top each slice with a heap of crab mixture, garnish with parsley and serve hot!

CRAB CORDON BLEU

Serves 4-6

2 cups cooked crabmeat
1 cup BECHAMEL SAUCE
  (see chapter 15)

1/2 cup crumbled bleu cheese
1 cup chopped lean ham
French bread, thinly sliced

In a large bowl, combine the crabmeat, BECHAMEL SAUCE, bleu cheese and ham. Arrange bread slices on a cookie sheet then spoon equal amounts of crab mixture over the bread. Place in a preheated oven set at 400 degrees and bake for about 15 minutes or until mixture is hot and bubbly.

CRAB STUFFED CREAM PUFFS

Serves 6-12

PASTRY
1/4 lb. butter
1 cup water
1 cup flour

1 teaspoon grated
   Parmesan cheese
4 eggs

FILLING
2 cups cooked crabmeat
1 cup heavy cream
1 teaspoon chopped
   fresh parsley

salt and pepper to taste

In a saucepan, heat the butter and water until the butter melts. Add the flour and grated cheese and beat vigorously until the mixture is smooth and comes away from the sides and bottom of the pan in one heap.

Remove the pan from the heat and set aside to cool slightly (about 5 min). After five minutes, add the eggs, one at a time, and beat each egg vigorously into the batter before adding the next egg.

Grease a large cookie sheet and drop spoonfuls of mixture in heaps onto the cookie sheet (about 2 inches apart). You should finish with 12-15 mounds of dough.

Bake in a preheated oven set at 450 degrees for 10 minutes. Reduce the heat to 400 degrees and continue to bake for half an hour longer. The cream puff pastries should have risen and browned. Set aside while you prepare the filling.

Keep the cream and cooked crabmeat chilled until you are ready to prepare the filling. It is also a good idea to chill the equipment used to whip the filling (no, don't put the electric mixer in the refrigerator...just the whipping attachments).

Beat the cream until it is light and fluffy and doubled in bulk. Stir in the crabmeat, parsley, salt and pepper. Cut each pastry lengthwise and slightly above center. Fill the bottom of each pastry with a dollop of creamed crab, then press each pastry top lightly over the crab. Serve immediately with a chilled filling and a warm pastry.

ANGUILLES EN BIERE

Serves 4-6

(eels in beer)

This dish came from the hop-growing northern regions of France where the climate is unfavorable for growing grapes. Beer, instead of wine, is used to flavor the food.

**2 lbs. eels,
    cleaned and skinned**
1/4 lb. butter (1 stick)
1 quart flat, warm beer or ale
1 bay leaf

1/2 teaspoon thyme
1/2 teaspoon rosemary
1/4 cup parsley
pinch of nutmeg
salt and pepper to taste

Cut the eels into 2-inch pieces. Heat up a large frypan then add the butter. When the butter begins to foam, add the eel pieces and fry on all sides until lightly browned. Pour in the beer. Tie the bay leaf, thyme and rosemary in a wad of cheesecloth (bouquet garni) and add to the frypan. Add the nutmeg, salt and pepper. Continue to simmer for half an hour. Remove from the heat and stir in the parsley. Serve hot with toasted French bread.

MUSSELS IN SHERRY

Serves 4-6

2 dozen fresh mussels
2 cups sherry (the good
stuff, not cooking sherry)

crushed hot red pepper
OLIVE OIL MAYONNAISE
(see chapter 15)

Scrub and debeard the mussels then spread them in a large shallow pan. Pour the wine over the mussels, cover the pot and cook over high heat for about 5 minutes or until all the mussels have opened.

Arrange the mussels on a large platter. Pull off each top shell and discard. Sprinkle a dash of hot red pepper over each mussel then top each with a dollop of OLIVE OIL MAYONNAISE. Serve hot!

CHAPTER 5

AN ITALIAN KITCHEN

by
AGLIANO

Sal

COOKING·WITH
Sal

5

AN ITALIAN KITCHEN

At about the turn of the century, my dear grandmother Luisa sailed across the Atlantic from Naples, Italy with hopes of finding a better life here in the United States. She brought with her into the New World nothing more than a hat, a print dress, a sack of flour, two plump chickens, and a lifetime of Old World customs and traditions.

The flour was soon kneaded into bread, the chickens boiled into soup, and were eaten. Soon after, the hat and dress wore out and were replaced. But Luisa's Old World ways endured unwaveringly throughout the rest of her life. This was true of many of the Italian immigrants of that era.

One thing I remember about these Old World Italians is that they demanded huge cooking areas. When I was growing up in Brooklyn during the 40's and 50's, the kitchen was the most important room in the house. It was the axis by which Italian families revolved. It was, of course, the cooking area. But more than that it was the family room, the recreation room, the conference room, and the room in which to receive and entertain guests—usually with a bite to eat and a steaming hot cup of Italian black coffee.

The Italian kitchen was a busy, crowded place from dawn to dusk as classic Italian dishes were prepared to perfection— and I might add, from scratch using the most basic of equipment. Many of the seafood dishes featured in this chapter evolved from such humble beginnings.

CRAB AND LINGUINE
Serves 4-6
(TRADITIONAL)

1 lb. linguine
8-12 blue crabs, live

2 quarts SEAFOOD PASTA
SAUCE (see chapter 15)

Prepare the SEAFOOD PASTA SAUCE as described in chapter 15. After the sauce has simmered for two hours, stab kill the crabs, clean them, split the bodies in half and detach the claws. Add the crab sections to the sauce and continue to simmer, stirring frequently, for an additional hour.

Half an hour before the sauce is done, fill a large kettle with water to the three-quarter mark. Add a teaspoon of salt and a tablespoon of oil (these help to keep the pasta from sticking and the water from foaming). Heat until the water reaches a rolling boil. Add the linguine and cook until desired tenderness is reached, stirring frequently.

When done, drain the pasta thoroughly then heap on a large platter. Pick out the crab sections and arrange them around the pasta. Top with generous amounts of sauce. Sprinkle on grated Parmesan cheese and garnish with snips of fresh basil. Serve hot!

CRAB AND LINGUINE AL PESTO

Serves 4-6

1 lb. linguine
8-12 blue crabs, live
1/2 cup olive oil
2 cups fresh basil leaves
6 cloves garlic

2 tablespoons pine nuts
 (pignoli)
2 tablespons grated
 Parmesan cheese
2 mint leaves
salt and pepper to taste

Stab and kill crabs, clean them, split the bodies in half and detach the claws. Fill a large kettle with water to the three-quarter mark. Add a teaspoon of salt and a tablespoon of oil; heat until the water reaches a rolling boil. Add the crabs and linguine together. Cook until linguine reaches desired tenderness.

While linguine and crabs are cooking, prepare the Pesto. In a blender or food processor, combine the oil, basil, garlic, pine nuts, Parmesan cheese, mint leaves, salt and pepper. Puree at high speed.

Drain the linguine and crabs thoroughly then heap on a large platter. Pour on the Pesto and toss lightly. Serve hot!

PASTA E PESCE NEGRO

Serves 4-6

**1 lb. conchigliette
(small pasta shells)
1 lb. blackfish fillets**

**2 quarts SEAFOOD PASTA
SAUCE (see chapter 15)**

Prepare the SEAFOOD PASTA SAUCE as described in chapter 15. After the sauce has cooked for two hours, add the fillets and continue simmering gently for an additional hour; stir frequently but gently to avoid tearing apart the fillets.

Half an hour before the sauce is done, cook the pasta, then drain and heap on a platter. Arrange the fillets around the pasta. Top with sauce and grated Parmesan cheese. Garnish with snips of basil. Serve hot!

CHICKEN SEAFOOD CACCIATORE

Serves 4-6

**2 chicken breasts
2 cups crabmeat
1 cup baby shrimp**

**2 quarts SEAFOOD PASTA
SAUCE (see chapter 15)**

Strip the meat from the chicken breasts and cut it into strips. Prepare the SEAFOOD PASTA SAUCE, adding the chicken as soon as the sauce ingredients are assembled in the kettle. An hour before the sauce is done, add the crab and baby shrimp. Continue to simmer for an additional hour. Serve with a side dish of your favorite pasta or boiled rice.

STUFFED SQUID
WITH LINGUINE

Serves 4-8

Squid and octopus need only brief cooking to ensure tenderness. Once cooking has progressed beyond that period of time, it is necessary to prolong cooking to moisten and tenderize again. This dish is a classic example of such a technique.

1 lb. linguine	**1 cup bread crumbs**
1 lb. squid, cleaned with hoods intact	**2 cloves garlic, minced**
	1 teaspoon parsley
1 quarts SEAFOOD PASTA SAUCE (see chapter 15)	**1 tablespoon olive oil**
	salt and pepper to taste

In a bowl, combine the bread crumbs, garlic, parsley, salt and pepper. Mix until thoroughly blended. Stuff the mixture into the squid's hoods to within half an inch of the opening. Using roasting cord, tie the openings to lock the stuffing—no need to explain knots to fishermen!

Prepare the SEAFOOD PASTA SAUCE and as soon as all the sauce ingredients are assembled in the kettle add the stuffed squid hoods and the tentacles. Simmer gently, stirring frequently, for 3 hours.

Half an hour before the sauce is done, cook the pasta as described in the previous recipes, drain thoroughly, and heap on a large platter. Remove the stuffed squid hoods from the sauce and arrange them around the pasta. Top all with additional sauce and grated Parmesan cheese.

CODFISH AND LINGUINE WITH OIL AND GARLIC

Serves 4-6

1 lb. linguine
1/2 lb. codfish fillets,
  cut into cubes
8-12 cloves garlic, whole

1 cup olive oil
1 tablespoon fresh
  chopped parsley

In a frypan, heat the olive oil, then quick fry the codfish cubes until lightly browned—no longer! Set the fried codfish aside.

Prepare the linguine as described in the previous recipes. Drain and heap on a large platter. Brown the garlic in the same oil where the fish were fried. Remove from the heat and pour the oil and garlic over the linguine. Add the fried codfish and toss lightly. Sprinkle on the parsley and toss again. Top with grated Parmesan cheese and crushed red pepper. Serve immediately—this dish becomes gluey if allowed to sit for too long a time before serving.

If there are leftovers, try the next recipe the following day.

LEFTOVER PASTA PIE

Serves 4-8

My grandmother Luisa, was a genius at turning leftovers into glorious next-day meals. This dish was one of her favorites. She prepared it in a huge frypan right on the stove. Halfway through the cooking the pie had to be flipped into a plate then returned to the frypan to be cooked on the other side. I never fully mastered grandma's technique, so I found baking the pie an easier approach. Leftovers from the previous recipes may be used in this dish.

6 cups leftover pasta, including sauce and meat　　**6 eggs, slightly beaten**
oil

In a large bowl, combine the pasta, sauce and meat (cut any fish, meat, or shellfish into tiny pieces). Add the beaten eggs and fold into the mixture.

Oil a deep dish pie pan large enough to hold all the ingredients. Bake in a preheated oven set at 400 degrees for about half an hour or until pie is set. Chill, cut into wedges and serve as either the main meal or a side dish.

CRABMEAT RAVIOLI

Serves 8-12

2 cups flour
2 eggs
1/4 teaspoon salt
1 tablespoon olive oil
water
1/2 cup cooked crabmeat
1/2 cup ricotta cheese
1 egg
2 tablespoons plain
  bread crumbs

1 tablespoon chopped
  fresh parsley
1 teaspoon grated
  Parmesan cheese
salt and pepper to taste
4 quarts SEAFOOD PASTA
  SAUCE (see chapter 15)
6 blue crabs, live

Sift the flour in a large bowl then add the eggs, salt and olive oil. Mix thoroughly and add enough water to form a smooth ball. Knead briefly on a well-floured surface until the dough is smooth and elastic. Cover the dough with a damp cloth and allow to rest at room temperature for about one hour.

While the dough is resting, prepare the filling and begin the sauce. Combine the crabmeat, ricotta cheese, bread crumbs, one egg, parsley, Parmesan cheese, salt and pepper in a large bowl. Mix thoroughly, cover and refrigerate. Prepare the SEAFOOD PASTA SAUCE as described in chapter 15, adding the crabs an hour before the sauce is done.

After the dough has rested for about an hour, divide it into four parts and roll each quarter into a sheet of about 1/8-inch thickness. Keep remaining sections of dough and any trimming wrapped in a damp cloth (this keeps the dough from drying out). Using a jar cover of about 3-inches in diameter, press out circles of dough. Dust the circles with flour and stack. Scoop up any dough trimmings and combine them with the next section of dough. Continue to roll out dough and press out circles until all the dough is used up. With a minimum of waste you should finish with about 6 dozen circles, enough to make 36 ravioli.

Spread out enough circles of dough to cover your work area. Brush water along the edges of the circles (this helps form a seal and binds the dough). Place about 1/2 teaspoon of filling in the center of each circle (make sure none of the filling lies along the edges of the circles—this may prevent the dough from sealing properly). Top each filled circle with another circle of dough evenly aligned with the bottom circle. Dip a fork into water then press the fork tines into the edges of the dough all the way around the ravioli to bind the top and bottom circles.

An hour before the sauce is done, fill a large kettle with water to the three-quarter mark. Add a teaspoon of salt and a tablespoon of oil. Heat until the water boils. When the water reaches a rolling boil, slip in the ravioli one at a time. Boil, covered, for about 30 minutes or until desired tenderness is reached.

Drain ravioli, heap on a large platter and top with sauce. Sprinkle on grated Parmesan cheese, black pepper and snips of fresh basil.

FLUKE PARMESAN

Serves 4-6

2 lbs. fluke fillet
1 cup bread crumbs
2 eggs, beaten
cooking oil
  (enough for deep frying)
2 quarts SEAFOOD PASTA
  SAUCE (see chapter 15)

1/2 lb. shredded
  mozzarella cheese
1/4 cup grated
  Parmesan cheese
1/8 teaspoon oregano
black pepper to taste

Prepare the SEAFOOD PASTA SAUCE using whichever seafood you wish to flavor the dish—I prefer mussels. While the sauce is cooking, fry the fluke fillets. Dip each fillet into the beaten egg, then coat on both sides with bread crumbs. Heat a large frypan add the oil to about an inch from the bottom of the pan. When the oil is hot fry the fillets until golden brown. Drain on paper towels.

Pour a cup of sauce into a baking pan. Arrange the fillets side by side over the sauce in the baking pan. Pour on just enough additional sauce to cover the fillets. Spread the mozzarella and Parmesan cheese evenly over the top, then sprinkle on the oregano and black pepper. Bake in a preheated oven set at 375 degrees for about half an hour or until sauce is bubbly.

FLUKE PARMESAN HERO: Follow the above recipe until the ingredients are about to be assembled in the baking pan. Instead of using a baking pan, arrange the fillets, sauce, cheese and spices over Italian bread, sliced lengthwise. Bake open-faced in a preheated oven set at 375 degrees for about half an hour or until sauce is bubbly.

SEAFOOD MANICOTTI   Serves 4-6

1 lb. manicotti tubes
2 quarts SEAFOOD PASTA
  SAUCE (see chapter 15)
1 cup ricotta cheese
1/4 cup shredded
  mozzarella cheese
1 egg, slightly beaten

1/4 teaspoon black pepper
1 cup cooked crabmeat,
  flaked finely
1/2 cup cooked baby shrimp,
  chopped finely
1/2 cup cooked lobster meat,
  flaked finely

Prepare the SEAFOOD PASTA SAUCE as described in chapter 15 using a variety of seafood for flavoring (crabs, squid, mussels, etc.). While the sauce is cooking prepare the filling: in a large bowl, combine the ricotta cheese, mozzarella, egg, pepper, crabmeat, shrimp and lobster. Mix until well blended, then refrigerate.

About an hour before the sauce is done, cook the manicotti tubes in salted, boiling water to which a tablespoon of oil has been added. When the manicotti are cooked to desired tenderness, drain and stuff with the filling using a pastry bag or a sausage stuffer. Pour about 2 cups of sauce along the bottom of the baking pan. Top with enough additional sauce to barely cover the stuffed tubes. Bake in a preheated oven set at 375 degrees for about half an hour or until sauce is bubbly.

Using a long spatula, carefully remove the manicotti, placing two or three on each plate. Top with some hot sauce; serve hot.

FLOUNDER PRIMAVERA

Serves 4-6

1 lb. flounder fillets,
  cut into cubes
flour
oil
1 lb. tricolor rotelle pasta
1/2 lb. broccoli florets
1 small zucchini, sliced

1/2 cup fresh mushrooms,
  split into caps and stems
1 cup VELOUTE SAUCE
  (see chapter 15)
1 tablespoon
  Parmesan cheese
salt and pepper to taste

Cook the pasta in salted water to which a tablespoon of oil had been added. While the pasta is cooking, heat a frypan, add about 1/2 cup of oil, dust the flounder in flour and fry the fish until golden brown. Drain the fish and keep warm.

Add the broccoli, zucchini and mushrooms to the frypan, cover and oil steam over a low flame for about 5 minutes.

When the pasta is cooked, drain and heap into a large serving bowl. Add the fried flounder and steamed vegetables. Pour on the VELOUTE SAUCE, Parmesan cheese, salt and pepper; toss lightly. Serve hot!

ZUPPA PESCE

This tasty seafood dish can be served by itself or with a side dish of pasta. But to me, the best part of the meal is when I dip crusty Italian bread into the sauce that remains at the bottom of the bowl after everything else has been eaten.

**2 quarts SEAFOOD PASTA
SAUCE (see chapter 15)**
12 clams, live
12 mussels, live
1 lb. large shrimp, cleaned

1/2 lb. sea scallops
**1 lb. squid, cleaned, the
hoods cut into rings**
1/8 teaspoon oregano

Prepare the SEAFOOD PASTA SAUCE as described in chapter 15. As soon as all the ingredients have been assembled in the kettle, add the squid pieces. About an hour before the sauce is done, add the remaining seafood and continue to simmer; stir frequently.

When done, pour into deep bowls, cover with plenty of sauce and sprinkle on oregano. Serve hot...and don't forget the Italian bread!

EEL IN TOMATO SAUCE

Serves 4-6

**2-3 black eels,
cleaned and skinned**
2 onions, diced

**2 quarts SEAFOOD PASTA
SAUCE (see chapter 15)**

Cut the eels in 2-inch pieces. Start the SEAFOOD PASTA SAUCE and as soon as the tomatoes have been added put in the onions and eel pieces. Simmer gently for 3 hours, stirring frequently. Great with a side dish of pasta!

BAKED EEL ITALIANO

Serves 4-6

**2-3 black eels,
    cleaned and skinned
1/2 cup olive oil
1/4 cup wine vinegar
water, enough to cover
    eels completely**

**1/2 teaspoon oregano
2 cloves garlic, sliced
1 teaspoon red hot
    crushed peppers
salt to taste**

Cut the eels into 2-inch pieces. Combine all the ingredients in a shallow pan and refrigerate for about an hour.

After an hour, place the pan in a preheated oven set at 425 degrees and bake the eels in the marinade for half an hour or until they're tender.

CODFISH PIZZAIOLA

Serves 2-4

**2 codfish steaks
    (4-6 ounces each)
1 lb. ripe plum tomatoes
olive oil
1/8 teaspoon oregano
4 cloves garlic, sliced**

**1 teaspoon fresh basil,
    torn in pieces
1 teaspoon grated
    Parmesan cheese
salt and pepper to taste**

Arrange the codfish steaks in a lightly oiled baking pan. Slice the tomatoes, then spread them out over the steaks. Sprinkle on the oregano, garlic, basil, Parmesan cheese, salt and pepper. Over all, dribble in a circular motion a fine stream of olive oil.

Bake in a preheated oven set at 475 degrees for about 20 minutes or until steaks test done.

CODFISH AND FENNEL

Serves 4-6

2 lbs. codfish fillets
2 large heads of fennel
2 cloves garlic
1 teaspoon capers
1 tablespoon raisins

1 tablespoon pine nuts
   (pignoli)
1/2 cup tomato paste
FISH FUMET (see chapter 15)
1/4 cup olive oil

Wash, then cut the fennel into chunks (use bulbs, stalks, and leaves); set aside in a colander to drain. Heat a large pot or a Dutch oven, then add the olive oil. Saute the fennel briefly, then add the garlic, capers, raisins, pine nuts, tomato paste and a cup of FISH FUMET. Simmer gently for about 20 minutes or until fish test done.

CODFISH AND BROCCOLI RABE: Prepare the same as the above recipe except substitute rabe (bitter broccoli) for the fennel.

CODFISH BASILICO

Serves 4-6

2 lbs. codfish fillets, cut
   into bite-size pieces
2½ cups fresh
   whole basil leaves
6-8 cloves garlic, sliced

1/2 cup olive oil
1 teaspoon red hot
   crushed pepper
salt to taste
juice of 1 lemon

Pour two quarts of water in a medium-size saucepan. Add 1/2 cup of basil and cook until the water boils. Reduce the heat to a simmer and add the fish fillets. Poach for about 10 minutes or until fish test done. Drain; discard the water and basil. Chill the fish, covered, in the refrigerator for about an hour.

After an hour, combine the chilled fish, remaining basil leaves, garlic, olive oil, red pepper and salt on a serving platter. Add the lemon juice, toss lightly and chill again for about an hour. Serve cold!

CODFISH POTATO STEW

Serves 4-6

1 lb. codfish fillets,
cut into chunks
3 medium-size potatoes,
peeled and quartered
1/2 lb. fresh string beans
4 plum tomatos, cored,
peeled, and quartered

2 cloves garlic, crushed
1/8 teaspoon oregano
1 tablespoon olive oil
2 quarts FISH FUMET
(see chapter 15)
salt and pepper to taste

Heat a large kettle, then add the olive oil. When the oil is hot, add the potatoes, string beans and garlic; saute briefly. Add the tomatoes and continue to cook, stirring continuously, for about 5 minutes. Lower flame to a simmer, add the oregano, FISH FUMET, salt and pepper, and simmer gently for about half an hour or until potatoes and string beans are slightly tender.

Add the fillets, continue to cook for an additional half an hour or until fish test done. Serve in deep bowls with plenty of crusty Italian bread for dunking.

BLUEFISH ALA SGUEGLIA

Serves 4-6

1 bluefish (about 2½ lbs.)
2-3 cloves garlic, crushed
1/4 cup chopped
fresh parsley
1/2 cup dried mushrooms
1/2 dry white wine

3 tablespoons softened butter
3 medium-size potatoes,
peeled and sliced
1/4 cup olive oil
1/2 cup milk
salt and pepper to taste

Scale and fillet the bluefish, leaving its skin on. Soak the dried mushrooms in the wine. After an hour, drain the mushrooms, chop and return them to the wine. Add the garlic, parsley, salt and pepper; set aside.

Parboil the potatoes for about 10 minutes. Pour the olive oil into a baking pan. Slip in the fillets and turn them over several times to soak up the oil, finishing up with the fillets skin-side down in the pan. Place the potato slices around the fillets. Pour the milk over all, then pour on the mushroom/wine mixture. Dot fillets with butter and bake in a preheated oven set at 425 degrees for about 20 minutes or until fish test done.

STEAMED FROSTFISH Serves 2-4

2 whiting or ling
(about 1 lb. each)
1/2 cup olive oil
1/4 cup wine vinegar
2 cloves garlic, crushed
1 tablespoon minced onion

1 teaspoon red hot
crushed pepper
1/2 teaspoon thyme
salt to taste
water

Prepare a marinade using the olive oil, vinegar, garlic, onion, red pepper, thyme and salt. Scale and gut the fish then remove the gills, leaving the heads and tails intact. Place the cleaned fish into the marinade, then pour in enough water to cover the fish. Chill in the refrigerator for about an hour.

After an hour, drain the fish and pour the marinade into the bottom half of a steamer. Add additional water (if needed) to reach just below the upper chamber of the steamer. Oil the upper chamber and place in the fish.

Bring the liquid to a boil and steam cook the fish for about 15 minutes or until fish test done.

Transfer the fish to a platter, spoon some of the steaming liquid over the fish and garnish with snips of fresh parsley. Serve hot!

CHICKEN SEAFOOD SCAMPI

Serves 4-6

2 chicken breasts
1 lb. jumbo shrimp,
  cleaned and deveined
1/2 lb. sea scallops
2 whole squid, cleaned,
  with hoods cut into rings
1/4 lb. butter

4 cloves garlic, sliced
2 tablespoons chopped
  fresh parsley
juice of 1 lemon
1/2 cup dry white wine
salt and pepper to taste
olive oil

Heat a large frypan, then add enough oil to coat the bottom of the pan. Remove the chicken meat from the bones and cut into chunks. Saute the chicken pieces until lightly browned and cooked through. Remove the chicken from the frypan and set aside on a warm platter. Add more oil if needed and continue to saute the seafood just until done. Transfer all to a warm platter.

Wipe the frypan and add the butter. When the butter begins to foam add about 2 tablespoons of olive oil. Saute the garlic until lightly browned. Remove the pan from the heat, cool briefly and stir in the parsley, lemon juice, wine, salt, and pepper.

Arrange the chicken and seafood pieces on a broiling pan Pour on the butter mixture and broil for about 5 minutes.

Transfer chicken and seafood to a serving platter and pour on the Scampi sauce. Serve hot!

BROILED DOGFISH

Serves 4-6

Dogfish, small members of the shark family, are often encountered by fishermen seeking more favorable game. But rather than tossing back the harmless yet menacing-looking creatures, take one home and try this tasty, easy to prepare, Italian specialty dish. The dogfish should be gutted immediately after capture, then packed on ice to ensure freshness and quality.

**2 lbs. dogfish fillets
    cut into cubes
1 cup dry red wine
1 tablespoon wine vinegar
1/2 teaspoon salt
water**

**1/4 cup olive oil
1 tablespoon crushed
    red hot pepper
1/4 teaspoon oregano
juice of 1 lemon**

Combine the wine, vinegar, and salt in a shallow dish. Add the dogfish cubes and pour on enough water to cover the fish. Cover with plastic wrap and chill in the refrigerator overnight.

The next day, drain off and discard the marinade. Place the dogfish back into the dish. Add the olive oil, crushed pepper and oregano. Toss thoroughly to coat the fish.

Arrange the dogfish cubes in a broiling pan, pour on the lemon juice and broil for about 10 minutes or until fish test done.

PICKLED BLACKFISH

Serves 4-6

2 lbs. blackfish fillets
   cut into cubes
1 quart red wine vinegar
2 cups water
2 tablespoons sugar
1 tablespoon salt
1 large carrot, crinkle cut
1 cup cauliflower florets
MORE red wine vinegar
MORE water

1 green bell pepper, cored,
   seeded and cut into chunks
1 red bell pepper, cored,
   seeded and cut into chunks
1 cup eggplant
   cut into strips
1 tablespoon red hot
   crushed pepper
2 whole cloves garlic

Soak the fish cubes in a solution of red wine vinegar, water, sugar and salt for 2 hours. Transfer to a large saucepan and simmer gently for 10 minutes. Drain the liquid and submerge the fish cubes in cold water for 5 minutes. Drain the cold water and set the fish aside.

Place the carrot slices in the top chamber of a large steamer; steam cook for 10 minutes. Add to the steamer the cauliflower, green and red peppers, eggplant and garlic. Steam cook for an additional 10 minutes.

Combine the fish and steamed vegetables in a large bowl. Add the crushed pepper and toss lightly. Prepare a solution of 3 parts vinegar to 1 part water, enough to cover fish and vegetables. Pour over fish and vegetables. Cover and chill in the refrigerator overnight before eating.

LOBSTER TAILS FRA DIAVOLO

Serves 4

4 lobster tails
2 quarts SEAFOOD
  PASTA SAUCE
1 tablespoon crushed
  red hot pepper
1 bell pepper, cored,
  seeded and diced

2 cloves garlic crushed
1 teaspoon fresh
  chopped parsley
1 teaspoon chopped
  fresh basil
2 tablespoons olive oil
salt to taste

In a large saucepan, heat the olive oil, then saute the garlic lightly. Add the SEAFOOD PASTA SAUCE, crushed pepper, bell pepper, parsley and basil. Simmer gently for 2 hours, stirring frequently.

After two hours, add the lobster tails and continue to simmer an additional hour, stirring frequently. Serve with a side dish of pasta!

CHAPTER 6

THAT LATIN FLAVOR

by
AGLIANO

Sal

Sal

6

THAT LATIN FLAVOR

When my middle son, Spencer, eyed amorously the girl of his dreams, Nina Cosme, living right across the street from our Brooklyn home, he wasted no time slipping a band of gold onto the third finger of her left hand.

Nina is of Puerto Rican heritage and not only did she become a devoted wife, and later a loving mother to my grandson Adam, but she was a bridge that brought two families of different backgrounds together. We learned about each other's culture, especially in the area of cooking. Recipes were swapped and we were soon whipping up and enjoying Spanish dishes such as ''Bacalao con Tostones'' and ''Calamares en su Tinta'' while Nina's folks became old hands at such Italian classic dishes as ''Lasagna'' and ''Eggplant Parmigiana.''

We also learned that although Nina's folks had a common bond of other Latins in as much as they are all Spanish speaking, they had their own distinctive cultures. At one time it was said that the sun never set on the British Empire. The same could be said today, although in not so profound a statement, that the sun never sets in the Spanish speaking cultures of the world. The influences of Mother Spain have reached far and wide, establishing her cultural hold on South America, Central America, the Caribbean, and parts of Asia. Even here in the United States, Spanish is becoming the second most widely used language.

Aside from language, Spain has also influenced the cooking of its colonial conquests. Yet, although the cuisine of all Spanish speaking cultures possess that inimitable Latin flavor, they each have their own distinctive style, whereby one could say, without reservation, that dish comes from Spain, or that dish comes from Mexico, or that dish comes from Puerto Rico.

PAELLA (Spain)

Serves 8-12

1 dz. little neck clams, live
1 dz. mussels, live
6 blue crabs, live
2 lobster tails
1 lb. jumbo shrimp, shelled and deveined
1 to 1½ lb. tube of Chorizo (Spanish Sausage)
2 lbs. chicken parts (legs, thighs, wings, breasts)
1/4 lb. boneless pork, cut into cubes
about 1 cup of olive oil
2 small onions, finely minced
4 cloves garlic, crushed
3 large ripe tomatoes, cored, peeled and chopped
salt and pepper to taste
3 cups raw long grain rice
1/4 teaspoon saffron
6 cups water
1 10 oz. package frozen peas, defrosted
1 cup sliced pimento
1 cup green olives, pitted and sliced
1 tablespoon capers
2 cups dry white wine

Stab kill crabs, clean them, then split the bodies and detach the claws. Cut the lobster tails into 2-inch sections. Slice the chorizo into 1/2-inch pieces. Scrub the clams and mussels and debeard the mussels. Set all aside. Heat a very large frypan. Add about 1/2 cup olive oil. When the oil is hot, fry the chicken parts until golden brown on all sides. Set aside on paper towels to drain. Next, fry briefly the shrimp, crab and lobster; drain. Fry briefly the chorizo and drain with other fried meats and seafood. Add additional oil as needed.

Discard the oil, wipe the frypan and prepare a Sofrito: add 1/2 cup fresh olive oil and fry briefly the pork cubes. Add the onions, garlic and tomatoes. Continue to cook for about 10 minutes, stirring continuously. Remove the pan from the heat and stir in the salt, pepper and saffron.

Pour the wine into a kettle large enough to hold both the clams and mussels. Place the clams and mussels over the wine, cover the kettle and cook over high heat for about 5 minutes or until all the shells have opened. Remove the kettle from the heat and set aside.

In a baking pan which measures no less than 14 inches in diameter and 1½ inches deep, heat the 6 cups of water just to the boiling stage (yes, do it right on the stove!). Slide the baking pan off the heat and stir in the sofrito and rice. Boil again, stirring continuously.

Place the fried meats and steamed shellfish over the rice. Scatter the peas, pimento, olives and capers over the meats and rice. Place the baking pan into a preheated oven set at 400 degrees and bake, undisturbed, for half an hour or until liquid has been absorbed and the rice is tender.

Serve hot right from the pan and into individual plates. You may also notice a light brown crust at the bottom of the pan. It's called pegao. Scrape it from the pan and add a portion to each plate—it is delicious!

CALAMARES EN SU TINTA (Spain)

Serves 4-6

2 lbs. squid, cleaned with
   ink sacs reserved
1/2 cup olive oil
1 small onion, chopped finely
2 cloves garlic, crushed
2 tablespoons chopped
   fresh parsley

1 teaspoon fresh coriander
2 cups cold water
2 tablespoons flour
salt and pepper to taste
3 cups boiled rice

Cut the squid hoods into rings, the tentacles into three or four pieces and the fins in half. Heat a medium-size frypan, add the olive oil, and when the oil becomes hot, briefly saute the onion and garlic. Add the squid, parsley, and coriander; saute until the squid are lightly browned. Add 1 cup of water, lower flame and simmer gently for about 15 minutes.

While the squid are simmering, use the back of a spoon to mash the ink sacs through a fine sieve over a bowl. Pour the remaining cup of water over the ink sacs and then mash out as much ink as possible. Add the flour to the extracted ink and water and whisk until smooth.

Once the squid have simmered for 15 minutes, add the ink, salt and pepper, and continue to simmer gently for 5 minutes, stirring continuously. Heap the hot rice onto a platter. Pour the squid and pan contents over the rice. Toss lightly. Serve hot!

SQUID AND CODFISH STEW (Portugal)

Serves 8-12

1½ lbs. squid, cleaned and cut into strips
1½ lbs. codfish fillets, cut into cubes
1 cup minced onion
1 bell pepper, cored, seeded and diced
3 medium size ripe tomatoes, cored, peeled and chopped
2 cloves garlic, minced
1/2 cup olive oil
1 tablespoon chopped fresh coriander leaves
1 cup dry white wine
1 cup FISH FUMET (see chapter 15)
salt and pepper to taste

In a large kettle, heat the oil, then lightly saute the onions, bell pepper and garlic. Add the tomatoes, coriander leaves, salt, and pepper; simmer for about 5 minutes. Add the squid, codfish, wine and fish fumet. Cover the kettle and simmer gently for about 15 minutes or until fish test done. Serve in deep bowl; top with fried bread cubes.

CODFISH WITH AVOCADO
(Puerto Rico)

Serves 4-6

2 lbs. codfish fillets
2 potatoes, peeled and
  quartered
2 hard boiled eggs, quartered
1 large onion, peeled and
  thinly sliced

2 avocados
juice of 1 lemon
salt and black pepper
olive oil

Boil the potatoes in lightly salted water for about 10 minutes or until just tender—not mushy. Drain the potatoes and rinse, then soak in cold water. Poach the codfish fillets for about 10 minutes in water; test for doneness. Drain the fish and chill in the refrigerator. After an hour, peel the avocados and remove the pits. Slice the avocados into sections, douse with lemon juice and toss lightly. Remove the chilled fish from the refrigerator and break the fish into flakes. Drain the boiled potatoes. Arrange the fish, potatoes, egg sections and avocado sections on a serving platter. Spread the sliced onion over all. Season with salt and pepper, chill for about an hour, then serve cold.

BACALAO CON TOSTONES
(Puerto Rico)

Serves 4-6

**2 lbs. codfish fillets, cut
    into chunks**
**2 plantains, peeled and slic-
    ed diagonally**
1/2 cup olive oil

**1 small onion, chopped
    coarsely**
2 cloves garlic, crushed
1 cup tomato sauce
salt and pepper to taste

Place the sliced plaintains into a bowl, cover with water, add
a pinch of salt and set aside. After 5 minutes, drain the
plantains and pat dry.

Heat a frypan, add the oil and when the oil becomes hot, fry
the plantains until tender. Drain the plantains on paper
towels. When they are cool enough to handle, flatten each
fried plantain slice with the back of a spoon and return to the
hot oil and fry again. Drain and set aside.

Poach the codfish in a shallow pan of water until fish test
done, about 10 minutes. While the fish are poaching, add the
onions and garlic to the oil used to fry the plantains. Saute
until lightly browned. Add the tomato sauce, salt and pepper,
and simmer gently for about 10 minutes.

Drain the codfish and place on one side of a serving platter.
Place the fried plantains on the other side of the platter. Top
all with the onion/tomato sauce. Serve hot!

CHICKEN AND CRAB WITH RICE (Puerto Rico)

Serves 8-12

8-12 crabs, live
2 cups raw rice
4 cups water
1 teaspoon salt
2 tablespoons Achiotina
(lard colored with Annatto)
2 cups shredded boiled
chicken

1/4 cup olive oil
2 cloves garlic, crushed
1 small onion, diced
1 bell pepper, cored,
seeded and diced
2 cups tomato sauce
salt and pepper to taste

Boil kill the crabs, clean, then split the bodies and detach the claws. Cook the rice with water, salt and Achiotina until rice is tender. Remove from the heat, cover and set aside until the water has been absorbed.

In a large frypan, heat the oil then lightly saute the garlic, onion and bell pepper. Add the tomato sauce, chicken, salt and pepper. Simmer for 10 minutes, stirring continuously.

Heap the boiled rice onto a large platter. Arrange the crab pieces over the rice and top all with the chicken/tomato sauce. Serve hot!

PESCADO CON HEUVOS RANCHEROS (Tex-Mex)

Serves 4

I took liberties with this old "South of the Border" standby by poaching fish along with the eggs in a spicy tomato sauce.

4 flounder fillets
4 eggs
1/4 cup olive oil
2 cloves garlic, crushed
1 small onion, minced finely
**1 bell pepper, cored,
    seeded and diced**

1 quart tomato puree
1/4 teaspoon oregano
2 tablespoons chili powder
1 teaspoon ground cumin
1/2 teaspoon cayenne pepper
salt to taste

Heat a very large frypan, then add the olive oil. When the oil becomes hot, add the garlic, onion and bell pepper; saute briefly. Add the tomato puree, oregano, chili powder, cumin, cayenne pepper and salt. Simmer gently for about half an hour.

Once sauce has cooked for half an hour, slip in the fillets and simmer for about 15 minutes. With a slotted spoon, gently remove the fillets from the pan and transfer to individual plates. Spoon some hot sauce over the fillets and set aside.

Carefully crack the eggs and gently slip them, one at a time, into the simmering sauce. Try to keep the eggs apart. Simmer the eggs gently for about 5 minutes or until set. Gently remove the eggs with a slotted spoon and arrange one egg over each fish. Top with more sauce. Serve hot!

SEA BASS WITH CORIANDER AND CUMIN (Mexico)

Serves 4-6

2 lbs. sea bass fillets, cut
  into chunks
1 cup milk
1 teaspoon cayenne pepper
1 teaspoon ground cumin
1/4 cup oil
1 small onion, peeled
  and diced

2 cloves garlic, crushed
1 bell pepper, cored,
  seeded, and diced
1/4 cup chopped fresh
  coriander leaves
2 cups tomato sauce
salt to taste

In a bowl, combine the sea bass fillets, milk, cayenne pepper and cumin. Toss and refrigerate for an hour. After an hour, drain the fish and discard the marinade. Pat fish pieces dry.

In a medium size frypan, heat the oil and lightly saute the onion, garlic and bell pepper. Add the tomato sauce, coriander leaves and salt. Simmer gently for about 10 minutes.

Place the fish pieces in a shallow baking pan. Pour the sauce over the fish and bake at 425 degrees for 15 minutes or until fish test done.

Serve hot over mounds of boiled rice.

SEVICHE (Mexico)

Serves 4-6

**2 lbs. fish fillets (fluke,
  flounder, sea bass, etc.)**
juice of 6 limes
1/2 cup olive oil
2 cloves garlic, sliced

1/8 teaspoon oregano
1/2 cup scallions, chopped
1/2 cup chopped pimentos
1 tablespoon Tabasco
salt to taste

Cut the raw fish into strips and place in a bowl. Pour on the lime juice, toss and refrigerate for about 2 hours. After two hours, add the olive oil, garlic, oregano, scallions, pimentos, Tabasco and salt. Toss lightly then chill again in the refrigerator for another hour. Serve cold!

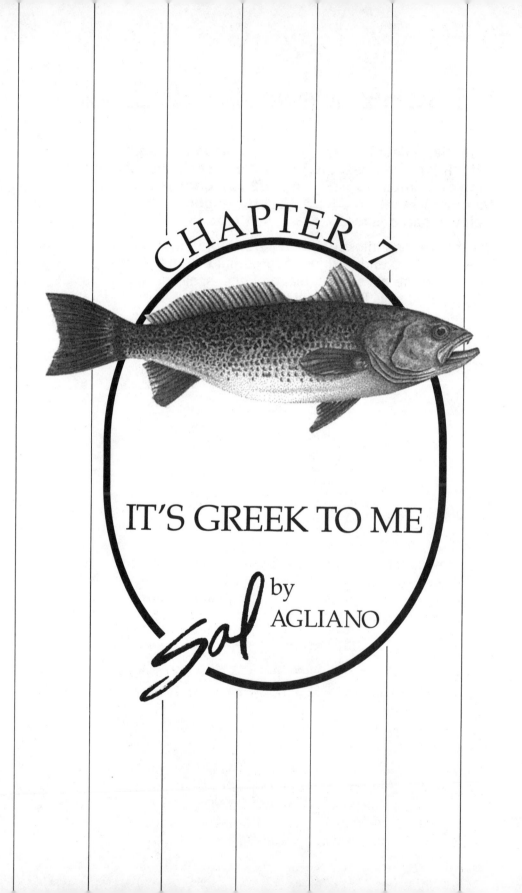

CHAPTER 7

IT'S GREEK TO ME

by
AGLIANO

Sal

7

IT'S GREEK TO ME

John the Greek, as he was called by the gang down in Sea Traveller's Marina in Mill Basin, is a huge, bulky-looking guy who fished regularly aboard my late brother-in-law Captain Paul Luisi's boat, Sailfin. John is over six feet tall, measures almost the same length from shoulder to shoulder, and has hands as big as bear paws. He also has an appetite which matches his physical attributes. Whenever he climbed aboard for a day of fishing, lugging a cooler of provisions, the rest of our party knew for certain we were about to partake of an on-board Grecian Feast. And although John usually devoured, by himself, more than half of the cargo he hauled aboard, there was always more than enough left for the rest of us—and then some!

But as they say: "Beware of Greeks bearing gifts!" For there was a catch to John's generosity—we had to put up with him constantly expounding the virtues of being Greek: The Greeks are the best fishermen in the world! The Greeks are the best cooks in the world! The Greeks are the best lovers in the world!

The first point was proven time and time again as John the Greek continually outfished us each and every time we took to water. The second point is proven beyond a shadow of a doubt by classic Greek recipes featured in this chapter. The third point...well, you'll have to discover that answer for yourself!

PLAKI

The concept, "Red meat, red wine; white meat, white wine," goes out the window with the preparation of this classic Greek dish.

2 lbs. fluke or flounder fillets
salt and pepper to taste
1/4 cup olive oil
3 onions, finely minced
2 leeks, finely chopped
2 cloves garlic, crushed
4 cups chopped tomatoes

1 tablespoon chopped fresh parsley
1/8 teaspoon oregano
1 cup red wine
1/2 cup Greek olives, pitted and sliced
2 lemons, thinly sliced

Sprinkle the fish lightly with salt and pepper and set aside in the refrigerator. In a large frypan, heat the oil and lightly saute the onions, leeks and garlic. Add the tomatoes, parsley and oregano; simmer gently for about 10 minutes, remove the pan from heat and stir in the red wine and the Greek olives.

Arrange the fillets along the bottom of a lightly oiled baking pan. Spread the lemon slices over the fillets, then spoon the tomato mixture evenly over the lemon and fillets.

Cover the baking pan with aluminum foil, poke a few holes in the foil and bake at 375 degrees for 45 minutes. This dish may be served hot immediately or cold the next day. Great with a Greek salad, some crusty garlic bread and a jug of wine—red of course!

FISH BAKED IN GRAPEVINE LEAVES

Serves 4

**4 small whiting (about
1/2 lb. each)**
1/4 cup olive oil
juice of 1 lemon
**1 tablespoon chopped
fresh parsley**

1 teaspoon thyme
1/8 teaspoon oregano
salt and pepper to taste
1 tablespoon anchovy paste
1/4 lb. butter (1 stick)
8-12 grapevine leaves

Scale and gut the whiting, removing the gills but leaving the heads and tails intact. Mix in a shallow pan the olive oil, lemon juice, parsley, thyme, oregano, salt and pepper. Roll the fish in this mixture, then cover and marinate in the refrigerator for about an hour.

After an hour, remove the fish from the marinade and pat dry. Cut the butter stick in half and mix one half with the anchovy paste until well blended. Spread the paste over each fish on both sides.

Parboil the grapevine leaves in lightly salted water for about 5 minutes. Drain the leaves, then wrap each fish in 3 or 4 leaves with the fishes' heads and tails exposed. Place wrapped fish, seam-side down, in a shallow baking pan. Dot with the remaining butter and bake in a preheated oven set at 375 degrees for about half an hour or until fish test done. Serve hot right from the oven!

FISH-STUFFED VINE LEAVES

Serves 4-6

1 lb. fish fillets (fluke,
   flounder, cod, etc.)
1 cup boiled rice
1/4 cup bread crumbs
1/8 teaspoon oregano
salt and pepper to taste
olive oil

1 small onion, finely minced
2 cloves garlic, crushed
1/2 cup fennel, finely
   chopped
4 cups chopped tomatoes
1/2 cup dry white wine
8-12 grapevine leaves

In a food mill or food processor, grind the fish fillets into a paste. Transfer to a bowl and add to the fish paste the boiled rice, bread crumbs, oregano, salt, pepper and 1 tablespoon of olive oil. Mix thoroughly then shape into a ball.

Heat a large frypan, then add enough olive oil to coat the bottom of the pan. Lightly saute the onion, garlic and fennel. Add the tomatoes and wine and season with salt and pepper. Simmer for about 10 minutes, stirring continuously.

Parboil the grapevine leaves in lightly salted water for about 5 minutes. Drain then arrange the leaves in pairs, overlapping one leaf over the other. Divide the fish mixture portions, one for each pair of leaves. Spread each portion over each pair of leaves, then roll up the leaves tightly and evenly.

Place the stuffed vine leaves, seam-side down, in a lightly oiled, shallow baking pan. Pour tomato mixture evenly over the vine leaves and bake in a preheated oven set at 375 degrees for about half an hour. Serve hot!

GREEK FRIED
SEAFOOD PLATTER

Serves 4-8

2 lbs. squid, cleaned with
   the hoods cut into rings
1 lb. jumbo shrimp, shelled
   and deveined
1 lb. sea scallops
1 lb. codfish fillets, cut
   into chunks

1/2 teaspoon black pepper
flour
cooking oil (enough for
   deep frying)
2 or more cups SKORTHALIA
   (see chapter 15)

Heat several inches of oil in a deep frypan. While the oil is heating, combine the squid, shrimp, scallops and cod in a large bowl. Add the black pepper and toss to distribute the pepper evenly over the seafood.

Spread the flour on a plate and roll the seafood pieces in the flour. Fry until golden brown (care must be taken when frying the squid; too long in the hot oil and the squid will become tough). Drain the fried seafood on paper towels, then arrange on a large platter.

This dish isn't Greek unless it's served with SKORTHALIA, a pungent Greek garlic sauce. The sauce is generally prepared ahead of time, chilled, and removed from the refrigerator the moment the frying is done.

Stab each seafood piece with a fork, dip it into the SKORTHALIA and enjoy!

RICE STUFFED SQUID

Serves 4-8

8 medium size squid, cleaned
with the hoods intact
1 small onion, finely chopped
1 cup boiled rice
1 teaspoon chopped parsley

4 cups chopped tomatoes
1/2 cup white wine
1/8 teaspoon oregano
salt and pepper to taste
1/4 cup olive oil

Coarsley chop the squids' tentacles and fins. Heat a large frypan, then add half the olive oil. Lightly saute the onions and chopped squid. Pour the pan contents into bowl and wipe out the frypan to be used later.

Add the rice, parsley, salt and pepper to the sauteed onion and squid. Mix until thoroughly blended. Spoon the mixture into the squid hoods, leaving enough space to tie the hoods shut with roasting cord.

Heat the remaining olive oil in the frypan. Add the stuffed squid and saute until browned. Turn each hood once during cooking—very carefully!

Remove the stuffed squid and set aside. Add to the frypan, the tomatos, wine, oregano, and season with salt and pepper. Simmer gently for 10 minutes.

Return the squid to the frypan and simmer in the sauce for about 40 minutes. Serve hot!

STUFFED FLUKE

Serves 4-8

2 fluke (about 2½ lbs. each)
1 10 oz. package frozen
  chopped spinach,
  defrosted
1/4 lb. Feta cheese, crumbled

1/2 cup bread crumbs
salt and pepper to taste
1 tablespoon olive oil
2 tablespoons butter

Fillet and skin the fluke, finishing up with one whole fillet from each side of each fluke. Drain the spinach, then squeeze out as much water as you can. In a large bowl, combine the drained spinach, Feta cheese, salt, pepper and olive oil. Mix thoroughly. Divide the mixture into four portions and spread one portion over each fillet. Roll the fillets, jelly-roll fashion, and secure with toothpicks. Place the rolled fillets, seam-side down, in a shallow baking pan. Pour about 1/2 cup water into the pan, then spread 1/2 tablespoon of butter over each rolled fillet.

Bake in a preheated oven set at 400 degrees for about 20 minutes or until fish test done. Top with BECHAMEL SAUCE (see chapter 15). Serve hot!

CODFISH WITH FENNEL

Serves 4-6

2 lbs. codfish fillets, cut
  into chunks
2 large heads of fennel
  (bulb, stalk, and leaves)
4 cloves garlic, crushed

1 small onion, finely
  minced
1/4 cup olive oil
1 cup red wine
salt and pepper to taste

In a large frypan, heat the olive oil and lightly saute the garlic and onions. Chop the fennel into chunks and add to the frypan; continue to saute until vegetables are limp. Add the wine, salt and pepper; toss lightly then place the fish over the vegetables. Cover and simmer gently for about 15 minutes or until fish test done.

CHAPTER 8

IF IT'S HOMEMADE,
IT MUST BE JEWISH

by
AGLIANO

Sol

8

IF IT'S HOMEMADE,
IT MUST BE JEWISH!

When I was about thirteen years old, for fifty cents a week I was given a piano lesson followed by a home-cooked Jewish meal. Each Wednesday, I arrived promptly at the home of Jazz musician, Artie Werner. Mama Werner always greeted me at a door with a stern face and a half-hearted gesture to enter. She was always busy in the kitchen, so I immediately went into the back room and practiced during the short time it took for Mama's son to arrive home from work. The lesson was short (only about half and hour), and before I could get my coat on, a plate was set at the table for me as if it were part of the fifty cent deal.

At first, I felt uncomfortable, as if I had been an intruder. Mama Werner spoke very little, and the little she did speak was in Yiddish directed at her son. My thoughts, however, were dispelled one day when I announced that I had to rush right home after the lesson and couldn't stay for dinner. Mama Werner actually looked disappointed! After an exchange of words with her son, she wrapped up some food in a brown paper bag and smiled for the first time I could recall, as she handed me the neatly-tied parcel.

As the weeks passed, my skills at piano playing improved and my interest in a new style of cooking (to me) was stirred. I no longer went into the back room, but stood by Mama as she prepared classic Jewish dishes such as Latkes, Chopped Chicken Livers, and Gefilte Fish.

Then one day, Artie called me at home to cancel that week's piano lesson—Mama Werner had died in her sleep that morning!

I'll never forget that dear, serious-looking but sweet, little old lady—even though I had only known her for a short time. If for nothing else, it was she, in her own humble way, who had enlightened me to a different, yet interesting, style of cooking.

SEA STYLE GEFILTE FISH

Serves 8-12

STOCK:

3 lbs. fish scraps (heads, tails, skin, and bones)

5 quarts cold water

2 carrots, cut into 2-inch pieces

5 large onions, sliced paper-thin

4 celery ribs, cut into 1-inch pieces

2 teaspoons salt

DUMPLINGS:

1 lb. codfish fillets

1 lb. blackfish

1 lb. flounder fillets

1 large onion, very finely minced

1 celery rib, very finely minced

3 eggs

1/2 cup matzo meal

1 cup cold water

1 teaspoon sugar

2 teaspoons salt

1 teaspoon black pepper

In a large kettle, combine the fish scraps and 5 quarts of water. Add a handful of salt and boil vigorously until the liquid is reduced by half. Strain the liquid through cheesecloth, discard the fish scraps and return the stock to the kettle. Add the sliced onions, carrots and celery. Simmer gently.

Between the simmering and boiling stages, prepare the dumplings. In a food mill or food processor, grind the fillets into a paste. Transfer to a large bowl and add the minced onion, celery and eggs. Mix thoroughly. Add the matzo meal, water, sugar, salt and pepper. Mix again until thoroughly blended. Cover and chill in the refrigerator.

After an hour, remove the dumpling mix from the refrigerator. Shape into potato size balls, then place the dumplings, one at a time, into the simmering broth. Cover the kettle and continue to simmer for half an hour.

Gefilte fish are best served cold the next day. Garnish with fresh parsley sprigs and serve with horseradish.

FISH BALL SOUP

Serves 8-12

4 quarts FISH FUMET
(see chapter 15)
2 lbs. mixed fish fillet (cod,
flounder, blackfish, etc.)
1 large onion, minced
3 carrots, sliced
3 celery ribs, diced

1 parsnip, sliced
2 cloves garlic, crushed
1/4 cup parsley, chopped
1 egg
1/4 cup matzo meal
1/2 teaspoon sugar
salt and pepper to taste

In a large kettle, combine FISH FUMET, onion, carrots, celery, parsnip, garlic and parsley. Season with salt and pepper; simmer gently for about 20 minutes.

While the vegetables are cooking, prepare the fish balls. Grind the fish fillets into a paste using a food mill or food processor. Transfer the paste to a large bowl, add the egg, matzo meal and sugar, then season with salt and pepper. Mix until thoroughly blended then chill until firm.

When the vegetables have cooked for 20 minutes, shape the fish mixture into balls about the size of small walnuts. Drop the fish balls into the kettle, cover the kettle and continue to simmer for about 30 minutes.

WHITING WITH APPLE SAUCE AND HORSERADISH

Serves 4-6

2 whiting
   (about 1 lb. each)
1/2 teaspoon salt
1 teaspoon cider vinegar
2 tablespoons butter

1/2 cup horseradish
1/2 cup unsweetened
   apple sauce
1/2 cup sour cream
salt and pepper to taste

Clean and scale the fish, then remove the gills. Leave the heads and tails intact. Blend the 1/2 teaspoon salt, vinegar, and butter, then spread mixture over the fish. Place the fish in a shallow baking pan and bake in a preheated oven set at 425 degrees for 10 minutes.

Blend the horseradish, apple sauce and the sour cream. Season with salt and pepper. After the fish has cooked for 10 minutes, pour the horseradish sauce over the fish and continue to bake 10 minutes longer or until the fish test done.

PICKLED SNAPPERS

Serves 4-6

12 snappers (about 7
   inches long)
2 tablespoons kosher salt
water
4 cups white vinegar
2 tablespoons sugar

1 teaspoon black
   peppercorns
1/4 teaspoon dill
3 large onions, sliced
   paper-thin

Scale then fillet the snappers, leaving the skins on. Place the fillets in a bowl, sprinkle on the kosher salt and toss lightly. Dribble in enough water to cover the fish. Set aside in the refrigerator for about an hour.

In the meantime, combine the vinegar, sugar, peppercorns and dill in a large saucepan. Heat to boiling, then lower flame to a simmer. Add the sliced onions, and simmer gently for about 15 minutes or until onions are limp. Remove from heat and set aside.

After an hour's chilling, transfer the fish and brine solution to a saucepan and simmer gently for about 10 minutes. Drain the fish and rinse under cold water. Add the fish to the vinegar mixture, mix lightly then transfer all to a large bowl. Cover the bowl with plastic wrap, then chill in the refrigerator overnight before eating.

FLOUNDER AND CREAMED CARROTS

Serves 2-4

1½ lbs. fluke or flounder
  fillets
3 carrots, shredded
1 tablespoon raisins
1 teaspoon dill

1/4 cup cider vinegar
water
salt and pepper to taste
1 cup sour cream

In a saucepan, combine the shredded carrots, raisins, dill, vinegar and enough water to cover the carrots by an inch. Season with salt and pepper and simmer gently for 15 minutes.

After 15 minutes, add the fillets (press them beneath the liquid or add just a touch more water to cover the fish). Cover the saucepan and continue to simmer for about 10 minutes or until fish test done.

Carefully remove the fillets from the saucepan and arrange them on a warm platter. Drain the liquid from the saucepan and add the remaining ingredients to the sour cream. Mix until well blended. Spoon over the fish and serve hot!

JELLIED FISH

Serves 2-4

**2 codfish steaks
(4-6 ounces each)
1/4 cup olive oil
3 cloves garlic, crushed
1 quart FISH FUMET
(see chapter 15)**

**juice of 1 lemon
1/4 cup chopped fresh
parsley
1/8 teaspoon dill
salt and pepper to taste**

In a large saucepan, heat the olive oil, then lightly saute the garlic. Add the FISH FUMET (be careful, the oil may splatter), lemon juice, parsley and dill. Season with salt and pepper.

When the water begins to bubble, lower the flame to a gentle simmer, then add the fish steaks. Simmer for about 20 minutes or until fish test done.

Place the fish into a deep serving dish. Gently pour on the liquid and refrigerate, covered, overnight. The next day enjoy the fish cold in its own jelly.

CREAMED PICKLED SNAPPERS

Serves 4-6

**2 cups sour cream
fish and onions from
previous recipe**

**1 cup of liquid from
previous recipe**

After you've chilled the fish from the previous recipe overnight, drain all but one cup of the marinating liquid. Combine the one cup of marinade with the sour cream and whip until smooth. Add the fish and onions and mix again until well blended. Chill overnight.

CHAPTER 9

HOT STUFF FROM THE WEST INDIES

by
AGLIANO

Sal

9

HOT STUFF FROM THE WEST INDIES

A dear, sweet black Jamaican lady, Marjorie Burrell, whom I had known for many years, was so overwhelmed by the freshly caught porgies I had given her one day that she decided to whip up for me one of her native dishes: Escoveitch (Escabeche).

Drenched in a superb blend of spices, the fried then pickled fish was one of the tastiest seafood dishes I had ever eaten. As I was smacking my lips to the final morsel of fish, I decided to top off the meal with one of three tiny peppers Marjorie had draped across the fish to garnish the dish.

"Don't eat the pepper!" she shouted in her melodic West Indian accent. "That's only for flavor."

Well, the warning came too late, for in one gulp, I had devoured the pepper—seeds, stem, and all! I felt like a fire-breathing dragon gone berserk! Marjorie rushed to my side with a tall glass of cold milk to put out the fire in my stomach and a wad of milk-soaked bread to be placed on my burning tongue much like a cold compress. Temporary relief came in moments, yet it was several days before I fully recovered.

Now whenever I think of West Indian cooking, two words come to mind almost immediately: HOT AND SPICY! But by recognizing which ingredients are for eating and which ingredients are for flavoring, they're not so hot as to burn your tongue off and not so spicy as to overpower the dish. Just enough to awaken your taste buds and set them dancing to a Calypso beat!

ESCABECHE

Serves 4

4 porgies or sea bass
  (¾-1 lb. each)
juice of 2 limes
1 tablespoon sugar
water
1/2 cup flour
1/2 cup oil
2½ cups water

2½ cups white vinegar
4 jalapeno peppers
1 carrot, cut into matchsticks
  (julienne style)
1 large onion, sliced
  paper-thin
2 whole cloves garlic
salt to taste

Scale, gut and behead the fish—leave the tails on. Place the fish in a glass baking pan and pour on the lime juice and sugar. Season with salt and add enough water to cover the fish. Cover the baking pan with plastic wrap and chill the fish in the refrigerator overnight.

The next day, drain the fish and pat them dry; discard the marinade. Heat a frypan and add the oil. When the oil is hot, brown the garlic to flavor the oil, then remove and discard the garlic. Dredge the fish in flour and fry until crisp. Drain the fish on paper towels.

In a medium-size saucepan, combine the 2½ cups of water and vinegar. Add the jalapeno peppers, carrots and onion. Season with salt and simmer gently for about 15 minutes or until carrots are tender.

Arrange the fried fish in a glass baking pan. Remove and discard the jalapeno peppers then pour the remaining saucepan ingredients over the fish. Cover with plastic wrap and chill the fish in the marinade overnight. Serve cold the next day!

RUN DOWN

Serves 2-4

When I first attempted to prepare this dish, I had only an inkling of the techniques of West Indian cooking. The recipe called for coconut milk, but after saving the liquid from a dozen coconuts I realized I hadn't nearly enough milk called for in the recipe. After picking the brain of one of my West Indian friends, I discovered, much to my chagrin, that the liquid found in coconuts was not coconut milk but coconut water. Coconut milk had to be extracted from the pulp of the coconut.

2 codfish steaks
(4-6 ounces each)
1 tablespoon cooking oil
2 large, ripe coconuts
1 large onion, sliced thinly
1 cup sliced pimento

1 celery rib, diced
2 cloves garlic, crushed
1/2 teaspoon thyme
1/2 teaspoon curry powder
1/4 teaspoon paprika
salt and pepper to taste

Split the coconuts and pour the liquid into a large bowl. Scrape out the pulp and shred it into the bowl. Add enough warm water to cover the shredded coconut; set aside.

After two hours, strain the liquid into another bowl; squeeze the shredded coconut to get every last drop of milk. Discard the pulp or put to another use.

In a large frypan, heat the oil, then sear the codfish on both sides. Remove the fish to a plate. Allow the frypan to cool, then wipe it out. Pour into the frypan the coconut milk, sliced onion, pimento, celery, garlic, thyme, curry powder and paprika. Season with salt and pepper. Heat to just boiling, then lower flame to a simmer and return the fish to the pan. Simmer gently for about 20 minutes or until fish test done.

Transfer fish to a platter. Cover fish with pan liquid and ingredients. Serve hot!

WEST INDIAN
CODFISH CAKES

Serves 4-6

1 lb. codfish fillets
1 cup chopped onion
1/2 cup chopped scallions
1/4 cup chopped chilipeppers
1/4 cup hot water

1/2 teaspoon thyme
dash curry powder
salt and pepper to taste
flour
margarine

Place the chilipeppers in a small bowl. Pour on the hot water and, with the back of a spoon, mash the chilipeppers; set aside.

Poach the fish in water for about 10 minutes or until fish test done. Drain the codfish thoroughly then flake into a bowl. Add the onions, scallions, thyme and curry. Season with salt and pepper then mix well. Drain the chilipepper water into the fish mixture; discard the chilipeppers. Add about a teaspoon of flour to the mixture and blend in until the mixture holds together. Shape into a ball and refrigerate for about an hour.

After an hour, pour flour onto a plate. Shape the fish mixture into patties and dredge in flour. Heat a frypan, then add enough margarine to coat the bottom of the pan. Fry the patties until golden brown on both sides. Add more margarine as needed. Drain on paper towels. Serve hot or cold!

FISH COO-COO

Serves 4-6

**6 small okra, trimmed and
  cut into 1/2-inch pieces**
2 cups water
1 teaspoon salt
1 cup yellow corn meal
**1 lb. codfish fillets, cut into
  bite-size pieces**

1 small onion, chopped
2 scallions, chopped
2 cloves garlic, crushed
4 cups chopped tomatoes
1 teaspoon vinegar
1/2 cup oil
salt and pepper to taste

Pour the 2 cups of water into a medium-size saucepan, add the teaspoon of salt and bring to a boil. Add the okra and cook until tender (about 10 minutes). Pour in the cornmeal in a slow, steady stream, stirring continuously with a wooden spoon. Cook until mixture is thick and smooth, stirring constantly. Pour the mixture into a lightly oiled baking pan, pat down and set aside.

Heat a large frypan, then add the oil. Lightly saute the onion, scallions and garlic. Add the chopped tomatoes and vinegar. Season with salt and pepper, then arrange the fish pieces over the tomato mixture. Cover and simmer gently for about 20 minutes or until fish test done.

Pour the fish and tomato mixture over the cornmeal. Serve hot!

SEAFOOD ROTI

Serves 6

PASTRY:
1 cup flour	2 teaspoons lard
1/2 teaspoon salt	ice water

FILLING:
1/2 cup cooked crabmeat	1 teaspoon salt
1/2 cup cooked lobster meat	1 potato, diced
1/2 cup cooked baby	1 teaspoon curry powder
shrimp, coarsley chopped	1/2 teaspoon cumin
1 cup dried yellow split peas	salt and pepper to taste
2½ cups cold water	

Sift the flour and salt into a bowl. Add the lard and with the tines of a fork blend the lard into the flour until the mixture resembles coarse meal. Add the ice water, one teaspoon at a time, and mix until dough holds together. Shape into a ball and set aside, undisturbed, for about half an hour.

Divide the dough into six equal parts. Roll each section of dough into a circle of about 6 inches in diameter. Heat a large ungreased skillet, then fry each circle on both sides until brown blisters appear on the surface. Stack the pastries with a sheet of wax paper between them and set aside.

Boil the diced potato in salted water until tender—not mushy! Drain, rinse under cold water and set the potatoes aside in a pan of cold water.

In a saucepan, combine the yellow peas, 2½ cups of water and 1 teaspoon of salt. Cook until peas are soft and the water has been absorbed. Transfer to a large bowl. Drain the potatoes thoroughly and add to the peas. Add the seafood, curry powder and cumin. Season with salt and pepper.

Stir mixture until ingredients are evenly distributed. Divide the mixture into six equal portions. Spread one portion over each pastry circle to within an inch of the edge. Roll the pastry circles loosely, then wrap each filled pastry loosely, but securely, in aluminum foil.

Place the wrapped Seafood Roti onto a cookie sheet and bake at 375 degrees for about 20 minutes or until hot. Serve immediately!

CRAB CURRY

Serves 4-6

12 blue crabs, live
1 large, ripe coconut
2 cups chopped scallions
1 tablespoon curry powder

juice of 1 lemon
1/4 cup oil
salt and pepper to taste

Split the coconut over a large bowl and drain the liquid. Remove the coconut pulp and shred. Add the pulp to the bowl, then pour on enough warm water to cover the shredded coconut. Set aside for about 2 hours.

Stab kill and clean the crabs, then split the bodies and detach the claws. Place the crab pieces in bowl, pour on the lemon juice and toss. Set aside in the refrigerator until ready to use.

After the coconut has soaked for two hours, drain the liquid into another bowl and discard the pulp. Set the coconut milk aside.

Heat a large kettle, then add the oil. Drain the crabs of lemon juice, pat dry, and add to the kettle with the scallions. Fry the crab pieces until they turn orange in color. Add the coconut milk, curry powder and season with salt and pepper. Simmer gently for 20 minutes. Serve hot over boiled rice!

BLUEFISH WITH GREEN SAUCE

Serves 4-6

1 bluefish (2½-3 lbs.)
4 cloves garlic, crushed
1 tablespoon capers, finely
  chopped
1/4 cup chopped fresh
  parsley
1/2 cup ground, toasted
  almonds

4 hard-boiled egg yolks
1/4 teaspoon oregano
1/4 teaspoon ground cumin
juice of 1 lime
1 cup olive oil
1/4 cup white vinegar
salt and pepper to taste

Scale, gut and remove the gills from the bluefish, leaving the head and tail intact. Season the fish inside and out with salt and pepper. Place the fish into a lightly oiled baking pan and bake in a preheated oven set at 425 degrees for 7 to 10 minutes for every inch of the fish's thickness.

About 15 minutes before the fish is cooked, prepare the green sauce. Combine the garlic, capers, parsley, ground almonds, egg yolks, oregano, cumin and lime juice in a food processor or blender. Season with salt and pepper and blend into a paste. Transfer to a bowl.

Pour in olive oil, one tablespoonful at a time, and whip after each addition until the oil is consumed.

Place the baked bluefish onto a platter. A moment before serving, add the wine vinegar to the green sauce and whip until smooth. Pour green sauce over the fish. Serve immediately!

SEATROUT BLAFF

Serves 4-6

2 lbs. seatrout (weakfish) fillets
juice of 1 lemon
2 cups dry white wine
1/2 cup chopped chilipeppers
salt to taste

1 onion, peeled and left whole
4 whole cloves
2 cloves garlic, crushed
1 bay leaf
1 teaspoon parsley
2 cups water

Pour the lemon juice and wine into a baking pan. Stir in the chilipeppers, season with salt, then submerge the fillets in the liquid; refrigerate.

Pour the 2 cups of water into a medium-size saucepan. Press the cloves into the flesh of the onion, securing the bay leaf with one of the cloves. Add the adorned onion to the water. Add the garlic and parsley and season with salt. Simmer gently for 15 minutes.

After 15 minutes, remove the onion with the attached cloves and bay leaf; discard. Remove the fillets from the marinade, then simmer gently for about 10 minutes or until fish test done. Serve the fillets on a platter; top with the liquid.

CONCH WITH RICE

Serves 4-6

2 lbs. conch, cleaned of
  viscera
juice of 4 limes
4 slices of bacon
2 tablespoons olive oil
1 tablespoon chopped fresh
  parsley

1 cup raw long-grain rice
1/4 teaspoon cinnamon
salt and pepper to taste
water

Soak the conch in the lime juice and refrigerate for about half
an hour. Drain the chilled conch, beat with a wooden mallet,
then cut into strips.

Place the conch into a very large frypan, cover with water
and add 2 additional cups of water. Cover the frypan and
simmer gently for about 1½ hours or until conch are tender.

While the conch are cooking, fry the bacon slices in a skillet
until crisp. Remove the bacon, then crumble it back into the
fat. Add the olive oil and set aside.

When the conch are tender, add the crumbled bacon with its
fat and the olive oil. Add the raw rice, pimento and cinnamon.
Cover and simmer gently for about 15 minutes or until rice is
tender. Remove from heat and stir in the parsley. Serve hot in
deep bowls!

CHAPTER 10

A TOUCH OF THE ORIENT

by
AGLIANO

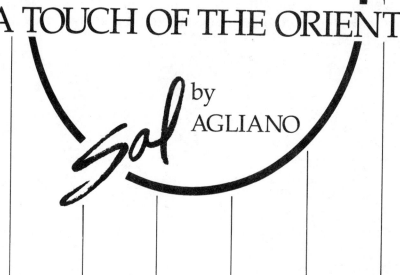

COOKING · WITH
Sal

10

A TOUCH OF THE ORIENT

David and Carol Kum were a father and daughter team who came to work for me in one of the restaurants I managed many years ago. They were Chinese, yet although we didn't prepare any Chinese dishes, David and Carol influenced me and my staff in the ways of Oriental efficiencies. Nothing was wasted, neither time nor food. If an easier way to do something was found, it was usually either David or Carol who had made the discovery. It was part of their ancient heritage.

One of the oldest culinary cultures in the world, Oriental cooking, as we know it today, evolved hundred of years ago as a result of a major fuel shortage. To preserve the precious fuel, foods had to be cooked quickly and efficiently. This led to the development of practical cooking utensils such as the bamboo steamer, the wok, chopsticks, and the Oriental cleaver, and time-saving cooking techniques such as stir-frying and multi-tiered steaming.

David and Carol Kum, as all other Orientals, continue to apply these practices no longer out of necessity but as tradition!

SEAFOOD EGGROLLS

Makes 12

The delicate skins used to prepare eggrolls and wontons can be purchased in many Oriental specialty shops. If you prefer to make them yourself, follow the instructions at the end of this recipe.

12 eggroll skins (see following recipe)
6 cups finely shredded cabbage
1 small onion, finely chopped
1/2 cup cooked crabmeat
1/2 cup cooked lobster meat
1/2 cup cooked baby shrimp
1/2 teaspoon cornstarch
1/2 teaspoon salt
2 tablespoons soy sauce

2 cups mixed Oriental vegetables:
bamboo shoots, cut in slivers
bean sprouts
black mushrooms, soaked then cut in slivers
water chestnuts, chopped
bok choy (Chinese chard), chopped
1/2 teaspoon fine-spice powder
oil (enough for deep frying)

Combine the crab, lobster, shrimp, salt and soy sauce in a bowl. Toss lightly. Add the corn starch, toss again, then refrigerate.

Boil about 3 quarts of water in a large kettle. When the water boils, add the shredded cabbage. Cover the kettle and continue to boil for 5 minutes. Drain the cabbage and squeeze out any excess water.

Heat a wok or a huge frypan then add enough oil to coat the bottom. Briefly stir-fry the onion and the Oriental vegetables. Add the drained cabbage, the seafood mixture and five-spice powder. Continue to cook 5 minutes longer, stirring continuously. Remove from the heat and allow to cool.

In a small bowl, beat the two eggs and 1/4 cup water. Spread the 12 eggroll skins over your work area. Brush the edges of the skins with egg mixture then heap equal amounts of stir-fried mixture in the center of each eggroll. Lift the bottom corner of each skin over the filling and press into place. Lift the two side corners slightly past the center and press into place. Gently roll the stuffed skin to the remaining corner. Brush all seams with egg mixture.

Heat about 4 inches of oil in a wok or frypan and fry the eggrolls, four at a time, in the hot oil. Turn the eggrolls in the oil until all sides are golden brown. Drain on paper towels. Serve with Duck Sauce, hot Chinese mustard or sweet and sour sauce.

STUFFING AN EGGROLL

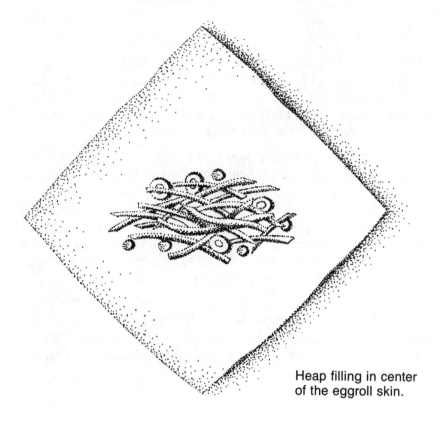

Heap filling in center of the eggroll skin.

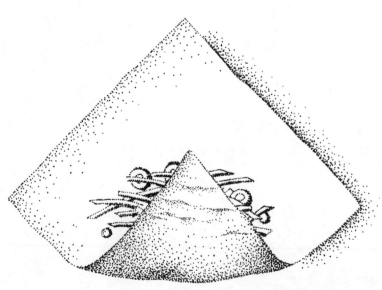

Fold the bottom corner over the filling.

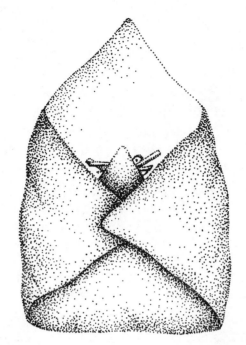

Fold each side corner
over bottom corner.

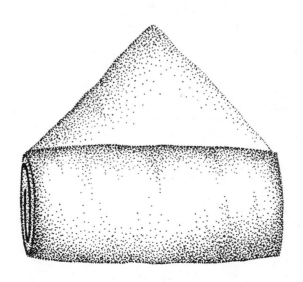

Roll up the eggroll
to the top corner.

EGGROLL/WONTON SKINS
Makes 12 eggrolls or 36 wontons

2 cups flour
2 eggs
1 teaspoon salt

1/4 teaspoon sugar
1 tablespoon oil
water

In a large bowl, sift together the flour salt, and sugar. Add the eggs and oil and mix until dough holds together. Add enough water (if needed) to bind the dough. Knead the dough on a floured surface until it's smoother. Cover the dough with a damp cloth and allow to rest for about an hour.

After an hour, awaken the dough by kneading briefly. Divide the dough into 4 equal parts and roll each section into a large sheet about 1/8-inch thick. Using a stiff carboard template measuring 7x7 inches, cut out as many skins as you can. Gather up any dough trimmings and add to the next batch of dough. Continue rolling and cutting out the skins until only a minimum of trimmings remain. You should finish with about 12 skins.

To make wonton skins, cut the eggroll skins into quarters, each skin producing four 3½ inch wonton skins.

CRABMEAT WONTONS

Makes 16

16 wonton skins (3½ inch
   squares)
1/2 cup cooked crabmeat
1 scallion, chopped very
   finely
1 teaspoon corn starch

1/2 teaspoon soy sauce
1/4 teaspoon oil (preferably
   sesame seed oil)
dashes of pepper and
   ground ginger

Spread the wonton skins over your work area. Brush the
edges with water. In a bowl, thoroughly mix the crabmeat,
chopped scallions, cornstarch, soy sauce, oil, pepper and
ginger. Divide the crab mixture evenly among the skins, placing
a heap of mixture in the center of each skin. Fold one corner
over the filling and align with the opposite corner. Press to
seal. Bring the two side corners to center and press to seal.
Brush the exterior of the stuffed wontons with water.

The crabmeat wontons may be deep fried in hot oil until
golden brown or simmered in a soup until tender.

CRABMEAT WONTON SOUP

Serves 4-6

2 quarts chicken stock
2 leeks, cut into diagonal
  slices
2 cups fresh, torn spinach
1/2 cup bamboo shoots, cut
  into slivers
1/4 cup mushrooms, cut
  into slivers

1/2 teaspoon corn starch
1/4 cup water
2 tablespoons soy sauce
2 blue crabs, live
16 crabmeat wontons (see
  previous recipe)

In a large kettle, heat the chicken stock to just a boil. Lower
flame to a simmer and add the leeks, spinach, bamboo
shoots and mushrooms. Simmer gently for half an hour.

Stab kill the crabs, clean, then split the bodies and detach
the claws. Add the crab pieces to the kettle. In a small bowl,
mix the corn starch and water until smooth. Add to the kettle
with the soy sauce and the crabmeat wontons. Simmer gently
for about an hour.

Stab kill the crabs, clean, then split the bodies and detach
the claws. Add the crab pieces to the kettle. In a small bowl,
mix the corn starch and water until smooth. Add to the kettle
with the soy sauce and the crabmeat wontons. Simmer gently
for about an hour.

ROLLED CRAB AND SHRIMP TOAST

Makes 12

12 slices white bread
1 cup cooked crabmeat
1/2 cup cooked baby
   shrimp, coarsely chopped
1 tablespoon honey
1/4 teaspoon ground ginger

1 tablespoon soy sauce
1/4 cup finely chopped
   scallions
1 egg, beaten
oil, enough for deep frying
sesame seeds

Trim the crusts from the bread slices then roll out each slice with a rolling pin until the bread is very thin and doughy to the touch.

In a blender or food processor, blend into a paste the crabmeat, honey, ginger and soy sauce. Transfer the paste to a bowl and add the chopped shrimp and scallions; mix thoroughly.

Spread the paste over the bread slices to within an 1/8 inch of the edges. Carefully roll up the bread evenly and tightly, jelly-roll style. Secure with toothpicks.

Heat about 2 inches of oil in a wok or frypan. Dip the rolled bread in egg to coat thoroughly, then dip on all sides in sesame seeds. Fry the rolled bread in hot oil until golden brown on all sides and crisp. Drain on paper towels and serve hot.

BLACKFISH IN "HOT" PEANUT SAUCE

Serves 4-6

2 lbs. blackfish fillets
2 eggs
2 cups flour
2 tablespoons honey

PEANUT SAUCE:
2 cups chicken stock
2 tablespoons soy sauce
dashes of ginger and dry
   mustard

juice of half a lemon
1/4 cup hot water
oil (enough for deep frying)

1 cup smooth peanut butter
2 tablespoons Tabasco
   (more if you like)

In a medium-size bowl, combine the honey and hot water; stir until honey has softened. Add the lemon juice and stir briefly. Cut the blackfish fillets into bite-size pieces and add to the honey mix; toss lightly.

Beat the eggs in a bowl and pour the flour onto a plate. Dip the fillet pieces into egg then dredge in flour. Heat about 2 inches of oil in a wok or frypan and fry the fish until golden brown on all sides. Drain on paper towels and keep warm.

In a saucepan, heat the chicken stock to simmer. Keep the flame low, then add the soy sauce, ginger and dry mustard. Simmer for about 5 minutes. Remove the stock from the heat and stir in the peanut butter and Tabasco until smooth and creamy.

Arrange the fried fish on a platter and pour the sauce into a serving bowl for dipping fish. Enjoy!

STEAMED SEA BASS

Serves 2-4

2 sea bass (1-1½ lbs. each)
1 teaspoon ground ginger
1/4 cup oil
2 cloves garlic, crushed
2 tablespoons soy sauce

1 cup sherry
2 leeks, sliced diagonally
1 celery rib, cut into slivers
salt and pepper to taste

Scale, gut and remove the gills from the sea bass, leaving the heads and tails intact. Make several shallow, diagonal cuts along each side of each fish. Place the fish into a baking pan then prepare a marinade. Pour over the fish the oil, soy sauce and sherry. Season with salt and pepper, then rub the marinade inside and out of each fish. Set aside in the refrigerator for about an hour.

Start water boiling in the bottom half of the steamer. Set a large heat-proof plate in the top chamber of the steamer. When steam fills the top chamber, place the garlic, leeks, and celery onto the plate. Cover the steamer and steam the vegetables until tender (about 10 minutes).

Place the fish over the vegetables, pour on the marinade and continue to simmer about 15 minutes more or until fish test done. Serve the fish with steamed vegetables. Pour the liquid over all.

STEAMED SEA BASS WITH TOFU AND YELLOW BEANS

Serves 2-4

The fermented yellow soybeans and the bean cakes (tofu) called for in this recipe can be bought in most Oriental specialty shops. Some supermarkets now stock these products in areas devoted to Chinese cooking. The yellow beans are sold in cans or jars, and the tofu either packaged or loose in water.

2 sea bass (1-1½ lbs. each)
2 cups fermented yellow beans
2 bean cakes (tofu)
2 scallions, cut in diagonal slices
1 teaspoon finely chopped fresh ginger
salt and pepper to taste
2 cloves garlic, crushed
1/4 cup oil

Scale and pan dress the sea bass, then make several shallow, diagonal cuts along each side of fish.

Boil water in the bottom half of a steamer. Set a large heat-proof plate in the top chamber of the steamer. When the upper chamber fills with steam, place the sea bass in the center of the plate. Spread the yellow beans around the fish. Cut the bean cakes in quarters and distribute them over the yellow beans. Sprinkle the ginger and scallions over all then season with salt and pepper. Steam cook for about 15 minutes or until fish test done. Transfer the plate as is to the table and onto a heat pad—be careful the plate will be hot, so use pot holders!

In a frypan, heat the oil, then lightly saute the garlic. Remove from the heat and pour the oil and garlic over the fish, yellow beans and tofu. Serve hot!

LEMON GINGER FISH Serves 4-6

2 lbs. fish fillets (fluke, founder, cod)
2 tablespoons soy sauce
1/2 cup saki or sherry
1/2 cup fresh ginger, sliced
dash or pepper
1/2 cup oil

6 whole cloves garlic
corn starch
1 cup chicken stock
1/2 cup candied lemon peel
1/4 cup candied ginger
juice of 1 lemon

Cut the fillets into bite-size pieces and place them into a bowl. Pour on the soy sauce, saki (or sherry), ginger slices and pepper. Toss lightly, then refrigerate.

After an hour, remove the fish from the marinade and pat dry. Set marinade aside to be used later.

Heat a wok or frypan, then add oil. Brown the garlic lightly then remove it from the oil and set aside. Pour corn starch onto a plate and dip the fish pieces into the corn starch until lightly coated. Fry the fish in the hot oil until golden brown. Drain fish on paper towels.

Drain the oil from the wok, leaving just a thin film. Add the chicken stock, candied lemon peel, candied ginger, lemon juice, fried garlic and the reserved marinade. Heat over a high flame until reduced by half.

Arrange the fried fish on a platter. Pour the liquid and pan ingredients over the fish. Serve hot!

PORGIES IN
BLACK BEAN SAUCE

Serves 2-4

4 porgies (¾-1 lb. each)
corn starch
1/4 cup oil
2 scallions, cut into slivers

1 teaspoon finely chopped
fresh ginger
2 cloves garlic, crushed
2 cups black bean sauce

Scale and pan dress the porgies, then set aside. Heat a wok or frypan and add the oil. When the oil is hot, lightly fry the scallions, ginger and garlic. Drain on paper towels.

Pour corn starch onto a plate and dredge the porgies in the corn starch. Fry fish on both sides until brown and the skin is crisp. Drain and set aside.

Drain the oil from the wok leaving a thin film. Pour the bean sauce into the wok; stir briefly. Return the fried scallions, ginger and fish. Cook for about 5 minutes, stirring frequently. Pour onto a platter and serve hot!

SEAFOOD EGG FOO YOUNG

Serves 4-6

1/2 cup cooked crabmeat
1/2 cup cooked baby
  shrimp, coarsely chopped
1/2 cup cooked bay scallops,
  coarsely chopped
2 scallions, coarsely chopped

1/2 cup mushrooms,
  coarsely chopped
1/2 teaspoon salt
8 eggs
oil

SAUCE:
2 cups chicken stock
2 tablespoons dark soy sauce
dashes of ginger and pepper

2 teaspoons corn starch
1/4 cup water

Flake the crabmeat in a bowl, then add the shrimp, scallops, bean sprouts, scallions and salt; toss lightly. Stir-fry the mushrooms in a drop of oil until limp; add to the seafood. Beat the eggs in a bowl and add to the seafood. Mix until ingredients are evenly distributed.

Heat a large skillet, then add enough oil to coat the bottom. Measure a cup of egg and seafood mixture and pour it onto the skillet. Tilt the skillet slightly in all directions to spread the mixture. When the eggs set at the edges, fold one end over the other with a spatula, then fold again corner to corner to form a small omelet. Fry on both sides until lightly browned. Add more oil and prepare additional omelets until mixture is consumed. Set the omelets onto a warm platter while you prepare the sauce.

In a saucepan, combine the chicken stock, soy sauce, ginger and pepper; simmer. Mix the corn starch and water until smooth then add to the saucepan. Simmer until slightly thickened. Pour sauce over omelets. Serve hot!

FISH TEMPURA

1 lb. fish fillets (sea bass,
   blackfish, fluke, etc.)
1 cup flour
2 tablespoons soy sauce

2 eggs
1/2 cup milk
oil (enough for deep frying)

SAUCE:
1/2 cup saki (or sherry)
2 tablespoons soy sauce
1 teaspoon sugar

1 teaspoon slice ginger
1 teaspoon orange peel

Prepare the sauce first then set aside at room temperature to absorb the flavors of the ginger and orange. Mix the saki, soy sauce, sugar, sliced ginger and orange peel. Stir until sugar is dissolved.

Mix a batter from the flour, soy sauce, eggs and milk. Set aside for about half an hour. Meanwhile, cut fillets into bite-size pieces.

After the batter has rested for half an hour, heat a wok or frypan and add about 2 inches of oil. When the oil is hot, dip the fish pieces into the batter then deep fry until golden brown. Drain on paper towels.

Strain the sauce discarding the ginger and orange peel. Arrange the fish on a platter, the sauce in a serving bowl. Dip the fish into the sauce.

FISH TERIYAKI

I often had trouble finding the sweet rice wine required to prepare this dish, so instead I substituted sherry and a little sugar—it worked out fine!

2 lbs. fluke or flounder
  fillets
1/2 cup soy sauce

1/3 cup saki
1/3 cup sherry
1 teaspoon sugar

In a small saucepan, combine the soy sauce, saki, sherry and sugar. Simmer while stirring until sugar has dissolved. Remove from the heat and cool to room temperature.

Cut the fillets into bite-size pieces and stir the fish into the cooled liquid. Chill in the refrigerator for about half an hour.

Preheat the broiler, then arrange the fish on a broiling rack. Brush with the marinating liquid. Broil the fish about 4 inches below the flame for about 5 minutes on each side. Brush often with the marinade during cooking. When done the fish should have a brown glaze. Serve hot!

SWEET AND SOUR FISH

Serves 4-6

MARINADE:

2 lbs. mixed fish fillets (sea bass, cod, fluke, etc.)
1/2 lb. medium shrimp, shelled and deveined
1 egg
1/4 cup corn starch

2 tablespoons oil
1 teaspoon ground ginger
1 teaspoon salt
1/4 cup water
1/8 teaspoon red hot pepper sauce

BATTER:

1 cup flour
1 cup water
1/4 cup corn starch

1 teaspoon salt
1 teaspoon baking soda

SAUCE:

1½ cups sugar
1 cup chicken stock
1 cup white vinegar
2 tablespoons sherry
2 tablespoons oil
1/4 cup dark soy sauce
1/2 cup corn starch
1/2 cup cold water

1 carrot, crinkle-cut in 1/4-inch pieces
3 small tomatoes, cored and quartered
1 bell pepper, cored, seeded and cut in slivers
1 cup pineapple chunks
oil (enough for deep frying)

First prepare the marinade: in a bowl, beat the egg, then add the corn starch, oil, ground ginger, salt, water and red hot pepper sauce. Stir briefly. Cut the fish into bite-size pieces (leave the shrimp whole) and add the fish and shrimp to the marinade. Toss and refrigerate for half an hour.

Next prepare the batter: sift the flour and corn starch into a bowl. Add the water, salt and baking powder. Stir just until smooth.

After half an hour, drain the fish and shrimp and stir into the batter until all the pieces of fish and shrimp are thoroughly coated. Heat a wok or frypan, then add about 3 inches of oil. When the oil is hot, begin frying the fish and shrimp. Pierce each piece of fish or shrimp with a fork. Let it stand a few seconds over the bowl of batter to allow any excess batter to drip off. Lower the fish or shrimp into the hot oil and with another fork gently slide it into the oil. Fry until golden brown. Drain on paper towels then keep warm while you prepare the sweet and sour sauce.

Steam cook the carrots and bell pepper until slightly tender; set aside. In a medium-size saucepan, combine the sugar, chicken stock, vinegar, sherry and soy sauce; simmer. Mix the corn starch and cold water until smooth. Add to the saucepan. Add the steamed carrots and bell peppers, tomato wedges and pineapple. Simmer gently until sauce becomes syrupy.

Arrange fish and shrimp on a platter. Pour the sauce and vegetables over the fish and shrimp. Toss lightly and serve hot!

STIR FRIED FISH

1 lb. sea bass fillets (scaled
  with skins left on)
12 mussels, live
2 teaspoons oil

1 teaspoon corn starch
2 teaspoons soy sauce
1/4 teaspoon pepper

VEGETABLES:

1 lb. bok choy (Chinese
  chard)
1/2 lb. snow pea pods
1/4 lb. mushrooms, sliced
2 leeks, chopped finely
1 teaspoon finely chopped
  fresh ginger

2 cloves garlic, crushed
2 tablespoons corn starch
2 tablespoons cold water
2 tablespoons dark
  soy sauce
1/2 cup chicken stock
oil

Scrub, debeard and shuck the mussels. Drain and place into a medium-size bowl. Cut the fish into chunks and add the mussels. Add the oil, corn starch, soy sauce and pepper. Toss and refrigerate for half an hour.

Separate the bok choy stalks from the leaves; cut the stalks into diagonal slices and chop the leaves. Remove the threads from the pea pods then steam cook the pea pods until slightly tender. Drain and set aside in a pan of cold water. In a bowl, stir the corn starch and water until smooth; set aside.

Heat a wok or frypan, then add about 1/4 cup of oil. When the oil is hot, briefly stir-fry the ginger and garlic. Remove and set aside.

Add fish and mussels to the wok and stir-fry until fish turn white. Remove and set aside.

Add more oil if needed then briefly stir-fry the bok choy stalks, mushrooms and pea pods. Add soy sauce, chicken stock and bok choy leaves. Stir in the corn starch mixture and return the fish, mussels, garlic and ginger.

Simmer while stirring until liquid is slightly thickened. Pour onto a platter and sprinkle on chopped leeks. Serve hot with boiled rice on the side.

SEAFOOD FRIED RICE

Serves 4-8

1/2 lb. cooked crabmeat
1/2 lb. cooked lobster
1/2 lb. cooked baby shrimp
3 cups cooked long
   grain rice
1 teaspoon corn starch
1/2 teaspoon salt

1/4 teaspoon pepper
2 eggs
1/4 cup sliced mushrooms
1 cup bean sprouts
2 scallions, sliced
3 tablespoons dark soy sauce
oil

Chop coarsely the crab and lobster, then combine them in a bowl with the shrimp. Add the corn starch, salt and pepper; toss lightly and set aside.

Heat a large wok or frypan, then add enough oil to coat the bottom. Beat the eggs in a bowl, then dribble into the hot oil. Stir vigorously to create threads until the eggs set—no longer (eggs should be moist). Remove the cooked eggs and set aside on a warm plate.

Wipe the wok, then add additional oil to coat the bottom. Add the seafood mixture, bean sprouts and mushrooms. Stir fry briefly. Add 2 more tablespoons of oil, then add the rice, scallions and soy sauce. Stir continuously until rice is evenly colored. Chop the cooked eggs and add to the fried rice. Toss until ingredients are blended. Serve hot!

SEAFOOD CANTONESE

Serves 4-6

2 lobster tails
2 blue crabs, live
1 lb. medium-size shrimp,
  shelled and deveined
1/2 lb. lean pork, coarsely
  chopped
4 scallions, coarsely chopped
1 celery rib, sliced diagonally

2 eggs, beaten
1 teaspoon salt
1/2 teaspoon pepper
1½ cups chicken stock
2 teaspoons corn starch
2 teaspoons cold water
2 teaspoons light soy sauce
1/4 cup oil

Cut the lobster tails into about 1-inch segments. Stab kill the crabs, clean, then split the bodies and detach the claws. Combine crab and lobster with the shrimp in a bowl and set aside in the refrigerator.

In another bowl, combine the pork, scallions, celery, salt and pepper; mix until well blended. Heat a large wok or frypan, then add the oil. When the oil is hot, stir in the pork mixture and fry mixture and fry for about 2 minutes, stirring constantly. Add the seafood and stir-fry for about 5 minutes.

Mix the corn starch and cold water until smooth. Add the chicken stock to the wok followed by the corn starch and water. Add the soy sauce and simmer gently, stirring continuously, until liquid has thickened slightly.

Dribble the beaten eggs over the wok ingredients and stir in until eggs have set and are evenly distributed.

Pour the Seafood Cantonese into a large serving bowl; serve hot with a side dish of boiled rice.

HOT 'N SOUR BASS SOUP

Serves 4

Several years ago while dining in a fancy Hunan restaurant in midtown Manhattan, I so enjoyed this dish for both its taste and presentation that I just had to recreate it at home. After many futile attempts, I finally hit onto something worthy of my efforts. Here are the results:

4 very small sea bass (each no longer than 7 inches)
1/4 lb. sea bass fillets, coarsely chopped
2 tablespoons light soy sauce
2 quarts chicken stock
1/2 cup mushrooms, coarsely chopped
1 scallion, slice diagonally
1 cup chopped fresh spinach
2 bean cakes (tofu), cut into ½-inch cubes
2 tablespoons corn starch
2 tablespoons cold water
1 tablespoon dark soy sauce
3 tablesoons white vinegar
2 teaspoons red hot pepper sauce

Scale, gut and remove the gills from the sea bass, leaving the heads and tails intact. Place the fish into a baking pan and pour on the 2 tablespoons of light soy sauce. Toss lightly then refrigerate.

In a medium-size kettle, heat the chicken stock to a simmer. Lower the flame and add the mushrooms, scallions and spinach. Simmer gently for about 15 minutes.

Add the chopped fillet, tofu, vinegar and dark soy sauce; continue to simmer 15 minutes longer.

Start water boiling in the bottom half of a steamer. When the upper chamber fills with steam, oil the bottom of the upper chamber lightly, then place the whole sea bass into the top chamber (if you are using a bamboo steamer, place the fish onto a plate). Steam cook for about 10 minutes or until fish test done.

While the sea bass are steam cooking, combine the corn starch and water and stir until smooth. Pour into the kettle of broth and simmer until the fish in the steamer are cooked.

Place each steamed sea bass into a deep bowl. Stir the red hot pepper sauce into the broth and pour broth and vegetables over the sea bass in each bowl.

To enjoy this dish to its fullest, break off a section of fish with your spoon then dip the spoon into the broth, scooping up bits of vegetable, tofu and broth to accompany the fish. Serve hot!

CHAPTER 11

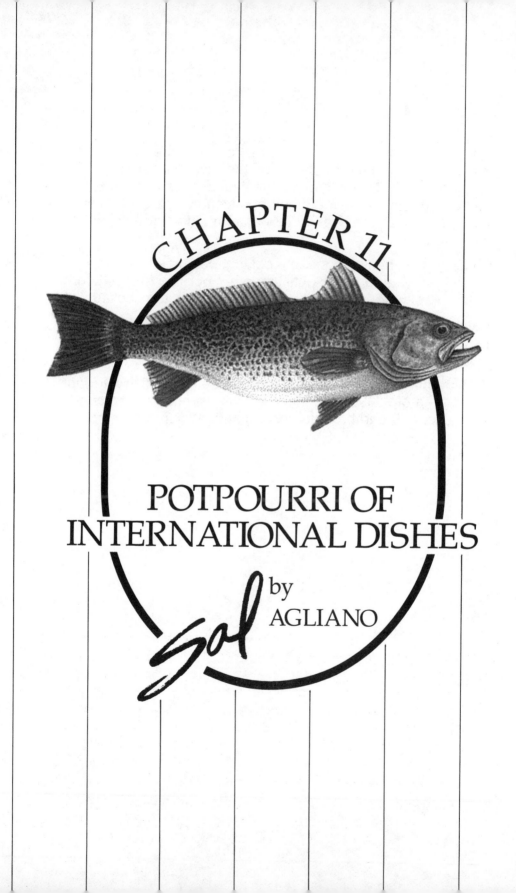

POTPOURRI OF INTERNATIONAL DISHES

by
AGLIANO

Sal

11

POTPOURRI OF INTERNATIONAL DISHES

Betty Harris is a grandmotherly English lady with an accent as thick as Yorkshire Pudding and a laugh as infectious as a dose of dentist's gas. To look at this jolly lady with the cherubic face and the devilish grin, you would think she didn't have a serious bone in her body.

But on the serious side, Betty is a frugal homemaker well versed in the art of English Cookery—seafood her specialty. And aside from all the tidbits of information Betty has shared with me over the years, it was she who enlightened me to the fact that although a recipe may call for a particular specie of fish, in many cases you could substitute one of several other types of fish and achieve satisfactory results.

To illustrate: one day Betty passed along to me a recipe in which the main ingredient was a particular fish called plaice. At the time I had never heard of this type of fish and asked Betty what it was and where I could get it. She said that plaice is a flatfish found in the English Channel, but I could use fluke in place of the plaice (pardon the pun). The dish turned out great and it got me to thinking about substituting many of our local fish in a variety of recipes calling for species I was either unfamiliar with or which were inaccessible. This lead to my whipping up dishes such as Fish 'n Chips using smooth dogfish taken while fluke fishing or spiny dogfish taken while codfishing, Bouillabaisse substituting sea robins and conger eels for the Mediteranean species, and Kerala using butterfish instead of the Indian pomfret.

In this chapter we'll do a little culinary globetrotting, venturing no farther than your favorite fishing spots while enjoying dishes from several different cultures around the world.

ENGLISH FISH 'N CHIPS

Serves 8-12

Fluke and cod fishermen may unsuspectingly hook into the main ingredient for this classic dish. Both the smooth dogfish of summer and the spiny dogfish of winter are used for fish and chips. As with all sharks, the fish should be gutted soon after being caught and packed on ice.

2 lbs. dogfish fillets, cut into cubes
4 cups cold water
1 cup malt vinegar (cider vinegar may be substituted)
1/2 teaspoon sugar
1 cup flour
1 tablespoon oil
1 egg, slightly beaten
1 cup warm beer
salt and pepper to taste
4 lbs. potatoes, peeled and cut French-fry style
cooking oil (enough for deep frying)

Place the fish cubes into a bowl and pour on the cold water and vinegar. Sprinkle on the sugar and toss lightly. Refrigerate for about an hour.

While the fish cubes are resting in the marinade, prepare the batter: in a large bowl, combine the flour, oil, egg, beer, salt and pepper. Mix just until smooth. Set aside to rest.

Heat enough oil in a frypan for deep frying (about 2 inches). When the oil is hot, fry the potatoes, a handful at a time, until golden brown. Drain and keep warm.

Drain the fish cubes and pat dry. Add the fish cubes to the batter and mix to coat the fish well. Pierce each fish cube with a fork, then hold it over the batter briefly to allow any excess batter to drip off. With another fork slide the fish into the hot oil and fry until golden brown on all sides.

Drain, then arrange the fish and chips on a large platter. Instead of lemon, the English sprinkle on salt and pepper and a little vinegar.

CURRIED MACKEREL
(India)

Serves 4-6

2 mackerel (about 1 lb. each)
2 teaspoons salt
1 teaspoon curry powder
1/4 teaspoon cayenne pepper
1 cup white vinegar
1/2 teaspoon sugar
1/2 cup oil

2 cups chopped onions
1 teaspoon finely chopped
  fresh ginger
6 cloves garlic, crushed
1 teaspoon chopped
  chilipeppers
water

Pad dress the mackerel, then place them into a baking pan. Pour on the salt, curry powder, cayenne pepper, vinegar and sugar. Rub the fish, inside and out, with the marinade, then chill in the refrigerator for about an hour.

In a food processor or blender, combine the onions, ginger, garlic and chilipeppers. Blend briefly just to chop finely. Heat the oil in a large frypan. Add the onion mixture and fry briefly. Place the fish over the fried mixture then add enough water to cover the fish. Simmer gently for about 20 minutes or until fish test done. Serve hot!

GERMAN-STYLE FISH AND POTATOES

Serves 4-6

2 lbs. codfish fillets
4 cups hot mashed potatoes
1/8 lb. butter (1/2 stick)
1 large onion, diced

1/2 teaspoon anchovy paste
2 teaspoons Dijon mustard
1 sour pickle, thinly sliced
salt and pepper to taste

Poach the fish lightly in salted water until fish test done. Drain, then flake the fish in a bowl. Add the mashed potatoes and mix until well blended.

Melt the butter in a medium-size frypan. Add the onions and saute until lightly browned. Stir in the anchovy paste and Dijon mustard. Season with salt and pepper; mix lightly.

Heap the fish and potatoes onto a large platter. Top with the onion sauce. Garnish with pickle slices. Serve hot!

FLOUNDER WITH BACON (Germany)

2 lbs. flounder fillets
juice of 1 lemon
salt and pepper to taste

6 slices bacon
2 cloves garlic, minced
flour

Place the fish fillets on a large platter, sprinkle on the lemon juice, salt and pepper. Toss lightly then set aside in the refrigerator.

Fry the bacon in a frypan until crisp. Remove the bacon and crumble it into a bowl. Fry the minced garlic in the bacon fat until golden brown. Drain on paper towels. Arrange the fillets on a platter. Sprinkle on the crumbled bacon and garlic. Garnish with lemon wedges and parsley. Serve hot!

MEDITERRANEAN SPICY PLATTER

Serves 4-6

1 lb. codfish fillets, cut
  into cubes
1/2 lb. medium-size shrimp,
  shelled and deveined
1/2 lb. sea scallops
1/4 lb. butter (1 stick)
1 teaspoon paprika

1 teaspoon ground cumin
1 teaspoon cinnamon
1/2 teaspoon ground cloves
1/2 teaspoon ground
  coriander seeds
salt and pepper to taste

In a medium-size bowl, soften the butter, then add the paprika, cumin, cinnamon, cloves and coriander. Mix until well blended.

Brush the fish, shrimp and scallops on a platter. Season with salt and pepper. Garnish with parsley and lemon wedges. Serve hot!

BONITO AND PEAS
(Mediterranean)

Serves 4-8

4 bonito steaks
  (4-6 ounces each)
1/2 quart dry red wine
water
1/2 cup olive oil
4 cloves garlic, crushed

4 cups chopped tomatoes
2 10-oz. packages frozen
  peas
1/2 teaspoon chopped fresh
  coriander leaves
salt and pepper to taste

Place the bonito in a baking pan, then pour on the wine and enough water to cover fish. Marinate overnight in the refrigerator.

The next day, drain the bonito, reserving the marinade for later use. Heat a large frypan, then add the oil. Lightly brown the garlic, add the tomatoes and coriander, and season with salt and pepper. Simmer gently for about 10 minutes.

Parboil the peas in lightly salted water until peas are slightly tender. Drain and set aside. Spoon enough tomato mixture to cover the bottom of a baking pan. Place the bonito steaks, side by side, in the pan. Spoon the remaining tomato mixture over the fish. Scatter the peas over the fish and sauce, then add enough marinade to cover the fish.

Bake in a preheated oven set at 425 degrees for about 15 minutes or until fish test done. Transfer to a platter and serve hot!

SCANDINAVIAN-STYLE PICKLED BLUEFISH

Serves 4-6

2 lbs. bluefish fillets (scaled
   with skins left on)
2 teaspoons kosher salt
water
4 cups white vinegar

2 cups sugar
1 tablespoon allspice berries
1 teaspoon black peppercorns
1/4 teaspoon dill
3 large onions, thinly sliced

Cut the fillets into 1-inch pieces and place them into a large bowl. Sprinkle on the kosher salt, toss, then add enough water to cover the fish. Set aside in the refrigerator for about an hour.

After an hour, combine the vinegar, sugar, allspice berries, peppercorns, dill and sliced onions in a medium-size saucepan. Heat to boiling, then lower the flame and simmer for about 10 minutes or until onions are limp.

Drain the fish and add to the saucepan. Simmer gently for 10 minutes. Remove the pan from the heat and set aside to cool briefly, then transfer the pan ingredients to a large bowl. Cover loosely with plastic wrap and refrigerate for an hour. After an hour, cover tightly with plastic wrap and chill overnight in the refrigerator. Serve cold!

CODFISH CAVIAR

16-24 canapé-size servings

2 cups codfish roe
4 cups cold water

1 cup kosher salt

Gently free the roe sac from the cod, then prepare to open the sac and separate the eggs. With a large rubber band secure a nylon mesh with 1/4-inch openings over a large bowl. Place the roe over the mesh and carefully cut the membrane from one end of the roe sac to the other. Peel off the membrane and allow the eggs to pass through the mesh opening and drop into the bowl. Measure off 2 cups of eggs and prepare the caviar.

In another bowl, combine the cold water and kosher salt. Stir until the salt has dissolved. Gently pour the eggs into the brine solution and allow to stand for half an hour. Mix gently occasionally.

After half an hour, drain the eggs over a plastic or stainless steel colander. Place the colander over a large pot and refrigerate for an hour, allowing the roe to drain completely.

After an hour, gently pour the eggs into small jars. Fill to the top. Cover and refrigerate overnight. Codfish caviar will keep for several weeks in a tightly covered jar left in the refrigerator.

CHAPTER 12

BACK IN THE GOOD OLD U.S. of A.

by
AGLIANO

12
BACK IN THE
GOOD OLD U.S. OF A.

What makes a particular dish truly American? After all, this country is considered a melting pot of many different ethnic cultures. New Orleans cooking, for instance, has been influenced by the French, Spanish, Portuguese, African, and Italian cultures, then spiced with native Indian and Caribbean cultures to develop what is now called Creole Cooking. Cajun Cooking of Louisiana was started by a band of oppressed Acadians (French Canadians) who fled the Northeast Atlantic and settled in Southern Louisiana because they refused allegiance to Great Britain. The cooking of the southwest states such as Texas, New Mexico, and Arizona brings to our lips that spicy flavor of Mexico. And the cooking of New England has remained faithful to the cuisine of the original English settlers.

But would you call pizza Italian; or chili Mexican because of their ethnic connotations? Probably so! Probably so! Yet although their roots are most assuredly ethnic, these popular dishes along with many of the seafood dishes featured in this chapter are so well entrenched in our culture, they are, without reservation, considered truly American!

NEW ORLEANS CRAB GUMBO

Serves 8-12

12-16 blue crabs, live
1 lb. chicken giblets,
  coarsely chopped
1 cup cooked ham, diced
6 ears fresh corn
5 quarts water
1 carrot, peeled and diced
3 small onions, finely
  chopped
1 cup celery, finely chopped
1 green pepper, cored,
  peeled and diced
3 cloves garlic, minced
3 lbs. fresh okra, trimmed
  and cut into 1/2-inch pieces

2 cups oil
1/2 cup flour
3 large tomatoes, cored,
  peeled and chopped
1 teaspoon thyme
1 teaspoon basil
3 bay leaves
1/4 cup chopped fresh
  parsley
1 teaspoon Tabasco
1/2 teaspoon Worcestershire
  sauce
dash of cayenne pepper
salt to taste

Stab kill the crabs, clean, then split the bodies and detach
the claws. Scrape the corn kernels from the cobs. Place the
kernels into a bowl and set aside. Combine the corn cobs,
crab pieces, bay leaves and 5 quarts of water in a large
kettle. Bring the water to a boil, then simmer for 15 minutes.
Remove and discard the corn cobs and bay leaves. Continue
to simmer the crab pieces very gently.

While the crabs are cooking, heat a large frypan then add 1 cup of oil (the remaining cup of oil will be used later to prepare a roux). Fry together the chicken giblets, ham, and okra until the latter exudes a sticky substance and has browned. Add the onions, celery, green pepper, garlic, tomatoes, thyme and basil. Simmer gently for about 10 minutes.

Scrape the frypan ingredients into the kettle with the crabs; continue simmering. In another frypan (you can use the same pan if you wash it thoroughly), prepare the roux (thickening agent): heat the remaining cup of oil over a very low flame then stir in the flour. Continue to cook, stirring constantly, until the flour assumes a deep brown color. Remove the pan from the heat and scrape the roux into the kettle of crabs and vegetables. Add the parsley, Tabasco, Worcestershire sauce and cayenne pepper. Season with salt and continue to simmer for half an hour, stirring frequently until the gumbo has thickened. Serve hot in deep bowls and over mounds of boiled rice!

CREOLE FISH ROLLS

Serves 4-8

2 fluke (1-1½ lbs. each)
1/2 cup raw long-grain rice
2 cups water
1 teaspoon salt
2 tablespoons margarine
1 tablespoon olive oil
4 cloves garlic, crushed
1 large onion, minced

1 green bell pepper, cored,
seeded and diced
6 cups chopped tomatoes
4 tablespoons Tabasco
2 tablespoons Worcestershire
sauce
1/4 cup chopped fresh
parsley

Fillet and skin the fluke so that you finish up with one whole fillet from each side of both fish. Refrigerate until ready to use.

In a medium-size saucepan, bring to a boil the cup of water with 1 teaspoon of salt added. Add the 1/2 cup of rice and boil for about 10 minutes or until the rice is tender. Remove the pan from the heat, cover and set aside until the liquid has been absorbed by the rice.

In a large frypan, heat the olive oil and margarine. When the margarine has completely melted, add the onion, garlic and bell pepper; saute briefly. Add the tomatoes, Tabasco, Worcestershire sauce, parsley and 1 cup of water. Simmer gently for about 20 minutes, stirring frequently.

Once the tomato sauce has cooked, measure one cup of the sauce and stir it into the boiled rice. Spoon another cup into the bottom of a glass baking pan. Spread the fillets over a work area. Divide the rice mixture into 4 equal parts and spread one part along each fillet. Roll the fillets, jelly-roll style, pushing the rice mixture in as it dribbles out (this is a loose filling). Secure the fillets with toothpicks and arrange, side by side, in the baking pan. Pour the remaining sauce over the fillets and along the sides. Bake in a preheated oven set at 400 degrees for about 20 minutes or until fish test done. Serve Creole Fish Rolls hot with plenty of sauce!

CAJUN FISH FRY

Serves 4-6

2 lbs. fish fillets (cod, fluke, flounder, etc.)
4 tablespoons Tabasco
2 tablespoons Worcestershire sauce
juice of 1 lime
flour
oil (enough for deep frying)

Cut the fillets into bite-size pieces and place them into a bowl. Pour on the Tabasco, Worcestershire Sauce and lime juice. Toss and refrigerate for about an hour.

After an hour drain the dish and roll in flour until thoroughly coated. Heat a frypan and add enough oil to deep fry the fish (about 2 inches). Fry the fish pieces in the hot oil until golden brown on all sides. Drain on paper towels.

Arrange the fried fish on a platter. Garnish with lime wedges. Serve hot!

STUFFED FLUKE: DIXIE STYLE

Serves 4-8

2 fluke (about 2 lbs. each)
1/2 lb. country-style roll
   sausage
2 tablespoons minced
   onion
1 tablespoon minced bell
   pepper

2 cups crumbled corn bread
   (home made is great!)
water (if needed)
1 teaspoon lemon peel,
   finely chopped
juice of 2 lemons
paprika

Fillet and skin the fluke so that you finish up with one whole fillet from each side of both fish. Refrigerate until ready to use.

Break up the sausage into little beads and fry in a frypan until lightly browned. Add the onions and bell pepper and saute until limp. Transfer the mixture to a bowl with fat from the frypan. Add the crumbled corn bread, lemon peel and just enough water (if needed) to bind the mixture (the fat alone may be enough to hold the mixture together).

Spread the fluke fillets over a work area. Divide the sausage mixture into 4 equal parts and spread one part over each fillet. Roll the fillets, jelly-roll style, and secure with toothpicks. Arrange the stuffed fluke, side by side, in a lightly oiled baking pan. Pour the lemon juice over the fluke and dust with paprika. Bake in a preheated oven set at 425 degrees for about 20 minutes or until fish test done. Serve hot!

SEAFOOD NEWBURG

Serves 4-6

1/2 cup cooked crabmeat,
   flaked
1/2 cup cooked lobster
   meat, coarsely chopped
1/2 cup cooked baby shrimp
1/2 cup bay scallops
1/8 lb. butter (1/2 stick)

1 teaspoon salt
2 cups HOLLANDAISE
   SAUCE (see chapter 15)
1/2 cup dry sherry
dashes of cayenne pepper
   and nutmeg

In a large frypan, melt the butter then briefly saute the crabmeat, lobster, shrimp and scallops. Transfer the seafood to a bowl.

Continue to maintain heat under the frypan as you add the sherry. Stir while cooking for about 2 minutes. Strain the sherry and pour over the seafood.

In the top chamber of a double boiler, and using as little heat as possible, prepare the HOLLANDAISE SAUCE as described in chapter 15. As the sauce thickens, add the seafood and sherry, cayenne pepper and nutmeg. Cook briefly while stirring until the sauce is smooth.

Serve Seafood Newburg hot over toasted bread slices!

NEW ENGLAND CIDER FLOUNDER

Serves 4-6

2 lbs. flounder fillets
salt and pepper to taste
4 cups apple cider
2 scallions, minced
1 clove garlic, crushed

2 tablespoons butter
2 tablespoons flour
1 tablespoon chopped fresh
  parsley

Season the fillets with salt and pepper then arrange them, side by side, in a baking pan. Dribble in the apple cider, then scatter the minced scallions over the fillets. Bake in a preheated oven set at 400 degrees for about 15 minutes or until fish test done. Transfer the fillets to a platter and keep warm. Strain and reserve 2 cups of pan liquid as flavoring for the sauce.

In a saucepan, heat the butter, then add the flour. Cook over a low flame, stirring constantly, until the flour has been incorporated into the butter. Add the 2 cups of pan liquid and cook, while stirring, until the sauce thickens. Pour the sauce over the fillets; sprinkle with parsley. Serve hot!

STUFFED WEAKFISH

Serves 4-6

1 2½-3 lb. weakfish
1 lb. cooked crabmeat
4 slices bacon
1/2 cup finely chopped onion
2 teaspoons finely chopped celery

2 eggs, beaten
1/2 cup bread crumbs
1/4 teaspoon poultry seasoning
salt and pepper to taste

Scale and remove the weakfish's bones through the stomach as described in chapter two. Rinse the gut cavity and chill the whole fish in the refrigerator until ready to stuff.

Fry the bacon slices in a frypan until crisp. Drain and crumble the bacon in a large bowl. Saute the onion and celery in the bacon fat, then add the sauteed vegetables and the bacon fat to the crumbled bacon. Add the crabmeat, beaten egg, bread crumbs and poultry seasoning. Season with salt and pepper. Mix thoroughly until the ingredients are evenly distributed and the stuffing holds together.

Pack the stuffing into the weakfish's gut cavity. Secure the belly flaps with roasting cord. Place the stuffed fish on a rack of a roasting pan into which about 2 cups of water have been poured. Bake the fish in a preheated oven set at 425 degrees for about 20 minutes or until the fish tests done. Serve hot!

STUFFED BOSTON MACKS

Serves 4-8

2 mackerel
  (about 1½ lbs. each)
1/2 lb. cranberries
1/2 cup bread crumbs
1/8 lb. butter (1/2 stick)

1 teaspoon anchovy paste
1 teaspoon finely chopped
  lemon peel
salt and pepper to taste

Scale, gut and remove the gills from the mackerel, leaving the heads and tails intact. Chop coarsely the cranberries in a food processor or blender. Transfer the chopped cranberries to a large bowl. Add the bread crumbs, butter, anchovy paste and lemon peel. Season with salt and pepper. Mix thoroughly until stuffing holds together.

Pack the stuffing into each mackerel's gut cavity. Place the stuffed fish in a buttered baking pan and bake in a preheated oven set at 425 degrees for about 20 minutes or until fish test done. Garnish with lemon wedges.

BLUEFISH LOAF

Serves 4-8

This classic American dish is usually prepared with salmon, but let's give our local bluefish a shot!

2 cups cooked, flaked bluefish
1 cup soft, cubed bread
1/2 cup evaporated milk (or half and half)
1/2 cup water
1 small onion, finely minced

2 eggs, separated
4 hard-boiled eggs, peeled and left whole
1 teaspoon soft butter
juice of 1/2 lemon
salt and pepper to taste

In a large bowl, combine the bread cubes, evaporated milk and water. Soak until the bread absorbs the liquid.

Add the bluefish, minced onion, egg yolks (no whites yet!), butter and lemon juice. Season with salt and pepper and mix until well blended.

In a clean, dry bowl, beat the egg whites with an electric mixer until stiff peaks form. Fold the egg whites into the fish mixture—don't overmix! Pour half the mixture into a well-buttered loaf pan (8½x4½x2½ inches) Arrange the boiled eggs in a row over the mixture. Pour on the remaining mixture to cover the boiled eggs. Bake in a preheated oven set at 400 degrees for about 30 minutes or until a knife inserted in the center comes out clean. Cool briefly, then unmold the bluefish loaf onto a platter. Garnish with parsley and lemon wedges. Serve hot or cold!

STEAMERS WITH BATH AND BUTTER

Serves 4-8

**2 quarts soft-shell clams
(steamers)**
1/2 lb. butter
2 cups minced onions

1/4 cup chopped parsley
dash of cayenne pepper
juice of 2 lemons
1 quart of hot water

Scrub the clams thoroughly, then place them into a large kettle. Add the onions and just enough water to line the bottom of the kettle (about 2 inches). Bring the water to a boil, then lower the flame to a simmer and cover the kettle. Simmer for about 10 minutes (don't let the water boil at this time). Remove the clams from the heat and pick out and discard those clams which failed to open. Place the opened steamers onto a large platter. Strain the liquid through cheesecloth and pour the liquid over the clams.

In a saucepan, melt the butter over a very low flame until it has liquified. Skim off the foam that has risen to the top of the clarified butter, then strain the butter into a warm serving bowl. Mix the lemon juice with the hot water, cayenne pepper and parsley. Pour the "bath" into another serving bowl.

To eat, remove the clam from the shell by the clam's toe. Dip the clam into the bath and swirl briefly, then dip into the melted butter. Enjoy!

FRIED SOFT-SHELL CRABS

Serves 4-8

4 soft shell blue crabs
1 egg, beaten
1/2 cup bread crumbs

salt and pepper to taste
butter

Clean the soft-shell crabs as described in Chapter Two. Dip the cleaned crabs into the beaten egg and coat with bread crumbs. Heat a large skillet and melt about a tablespoon of butter for each crab. Fry the crabs one at a time on both sides until golden brown and crisp. Drain on paper towels.

Serve the fried soft-shell crabs hot with lemon wedges and tartar sauce. Great as sandwiches served on hot crusty Italian bread!

GERRITSEN BEACH
FISH FRY

Serves 6-12

When I was about ten years old, I, and several budding fishermen of about the same age, spent a great deal of time fishing from the beach of a municipally-owned section of Gerritsen Beach in Brooklyn. No one was allowed on the property, but as long as we were only fishing and cleaned up whatever mess we made, the authorities looked the other way. The waters off Gerritsen Beach were abundant with several varieties of pan-size fish: snappers, porgies, lafayettes, flounder and an occasional feisty black eel. Many times the fish we caught were cooked over a primitive fire and eaten on the spot.

6 snappers, about 1/4 lb. each   12 baking potatoes
6 porgies, about 1/2 lb. each   butter

Using the tines of a fork, puncture many holes on all sides of the potatoes. Brush the potatoes with butter, season with salt and pepper and wrap tightly in aluminum foil. Place the potatoes directly onto hot coals of an outdoor fire or barbecue. Cook for about an hour or until the potatoes are soft, turning the foil-wrapped potatoes often. Remove the potatoes from the hot coals and set them along the exterior of the fire—just to keep them hot.

Scale and pan dress the fish. Brush the fish, inside and out, with butter, season with salt and pepper and wrap tightly in aluminum foil. Place the foil-wrapped fish directly onto the hot coals and cook for about 20 minutes or until fish test done.

Serve each fish hot with "Mickey" (baked potato) and eat with your hands the way we did back then!

FLOUNDER ROE PATTIES

Serves 4-6

1/2 lb. flounder roe
2 tablespoons finely
minced onion
2 eggs, beaten

1/2 cup bread crumbs
salt and pepper to taste
butter

Chop coarsely the flounder roe and place it into a bowl. Add the minced onion, beaten eggs and bread crumbs. Season with salt and pepper and mix until thoroughly blended. Shape the mixture into flat patties about 3 inches in diameter.

Heat a skillet and melt about 1 teaspoon of butter for each patty. Fry the patties on both sides until golden brown. Drain and arrange on a platter. Garnish with lemon wedges and parsley. Serve hot or cold!

CRAB RAREBIT

Serves 4-6

2 cups cooked crabmeat
1 cup BECHAMEL SAUCE
   (see chapter 15)
1 cup heavy cream
1 cup shredded cheddar
   cheese

1 teaspoon Worcestershire
   sauce
dash of cayenne pepper

Heat the BECHAMEL SAUCE, then stir in the heavy cream, cheddar cheese, Worcestershire sauce and cayenne pepper. Simmer until sauce thickens.

When the sauce has thickened and is smooth, stir in the crabmeat and simmer about 2 minutes longer. Serve hot over toasted bread!

FISH ON A BUN

Serves 4

No need to trek all the way to the local fast food joint to enjoy this classic American dish. Whip it up at home in your own kitchen.

4 flounder fillets (about 3 oz. each)
4 hamburger buns
4 slices American cheese
4 tomato slices
1 small onion, sliced paper-thin

2 kosher dill pickles
lettuce
4 tablespoons Thousand Island dressing
1 egg, beaten
1/2 cup bread crumbs
oil (enough for deep frying)

Dip the fillets into egg and coat with bread crumbs. Heat a frypan and add enough oil for deep frying (about 2 inches). Fry the fillets on both sides until golden brown.

While you are frying the fish, lightly toast the buns in the oven. Place one fillet over each bun bottom. Drape a slice of cheese over each fish and bake until the cheese melts.

While the fish and cheese are in the oven, dress the tops of the buns on individual plates with lettuce, tomato, onion and a dollop of Thousand Island dressing. Garnish with a half a pickle for each sandwich.

CHAPTER 13

IT'S PARTY TIME!

by
AGLIANO

Sal

13

IT'S PARTY TIME!

Whenever my wife, Dolores, and I plan a gathering in our home, we don't head for the closest caterer for meal preparations. No, we set out early in the morning shopping for all that we will need and begin preparations ourselves from scratch. Usually it takes the better part of the day to get all in readiness, but the end result justifies the extra toil.

We place as much emphasis on the appetizers as we do on the main course. And quite often the main course is overshadowed by our introductory snacks. We strive for attractive settings, garnishing the platters with radish roses, parsley clusters, and tomato rosettes. We also hollow out green, red, and yellow bell peppers to use as attractive containers for condiments such as ketchup or mayonaisse or for dips.

Seafood plays an important part in our preparations. Most seafood snacks are easy to whip up and provide a tasty overture to the main course. Check out the seafood snacks featured in this chapter for a more successful party setting.

CRABMEAT DEVILED EGGS

Makes 12

12 hard boiled eggs
1 cup cooked crabmeat
1 cup sour cream (or plain
** yogurt)**
1/4 teaspoon Dijon mustard
** (or horseradish)**

1/2 teaspoon sweet pickle
** relish**
salt and pepper to taste
paprika

Peel and chill the boiled eggs, then carefully slice each egg in half, lengthwise. Gently remove the yolks and set the hollowed-out egg white halves aside.

Break the egg yolks in a bowl. Add the crabmeat, and with fork tines or pastry blender, work the crabmeat into the egg yolks. Add the sour cream, Dijon mustard and sweet pickle relish. Season with salt and pepper and mix until thoroughly blended. Pack the crabmeat mixture into the hollowed-out egg whites. Cover with plastic wrap and chill for about an hour. Serve cold!

CRAB DIP

Makes about 36 canapés

1 cup cooked crabmeat
8 oz. cream cheese

1/2 cup half and half
1 tablespoon chopped chives

Combine the cream cheese and half and half in a bowl; whip until smooth and creamy. Add the crabmeat and chives and mix until well blended. Chill for about an hour before serving. Serve with saltines or wheat crackers.

CLAM DIP

Makes about 36 canapés

12 little neck clams, live
2 cups sour cream

1/4 cup finely chopped
fresh parsley

Steam cook the clams until shells have opened. Drain and shuck the clams (discard those which failed to open), then chop finely; chill for an hour.

Combine the chopped clams, sour cream, onion and parsley in a bowl. Mix until well blended. Chill for about an hour before serving. Serve with saltines or wheat crackers.

CRAB SOUFFLE

Makes 12

12 blue crabs, live
4 eggs, separated

grated Parmesan cheese
salt and pepper to taste

Boil kill the crabs and clean them without breaking the back shells—these will be used as baking cups. Crack the legs and body and extract as much crabmeat as you can. Flake the meat in a bowl and chill for half an hour.

Beat the egg yolks before blending them into the crab. Season with salt and pepper (not too much salt, the Parmesan cheese contains salt). Mix lightly.

In a clean, dry bowl, whip the egg whites with an electric beater until stiff peaks form. Fold the stiffened whites into the crab mixture—don't overmix!

Gently scrub the crab shells and place them onto a large, lightly oiled cookie sheet. Spoon the souffle mixture into the crab shells, heaping the mixture slightly. Sprinkle some grated cheese over each souffle. Bake in a preheated oven set at 400 degrees for about half an hour or until the souffles have risen and are golden brown. Serve immediately!

LOBSTER SOUFFLE

Makes 4

4 lobster tails
6 eggs, separated
2 cups BECHAMEL SAUCE
  (see chapter 15)

salt and pepper to taste

Poach the lobster tails in water for about 15 minutes. Drain and cool briefly. Cut the undershell from the lobster tails and remove the meat. Trim off any rough edges along the underside of the tail shells.

Chop the meat coarsely and place it into a bowl. Beat the egg yolks and mix into the lobster. Add the BECHAMEL SAUCE, salt and pepper; mix until well blended.

In a clean, dry bowl, whip the egg whites with an electric beater until stiff peaks form. Fold the stiffened whites into the lobster mixture—don't overmix!

Spoon the mixture into the lobster tails, heaping it slightly. Arrange the stuffed tails on a lightly oiled cookie sheet and bake in a preheated oven set at 400 degrees for about half an hour or until the souffles have risen and are golden brown. Serve immediately!

BAKED CLAMS SUPREME

Makes 12

12 chowder clams
4 slices bacon
2 cups cooked crabmeat (or
   a combination of crab,
   lobster and shrimp)
1 cup bread crumbs
2 eggs, separated
1/4 teaspoon poultry
   seasoning

1 tablespoon chopped fresh
   parsley
4 cloves garlic, minced
1 tablespoon grated
   Parmesan cheese
1 tablespoon softened
   butter
salt and pepper to taste

Fry the bacon slices crisp, then drain, crumble and set aside. Shuck the clams without breaking the shells—these will be used as baking cups. Chop the clam meat coarsely and, with its liquid, pour them into a bowl. Chop or flake the other seafood (crab, lobster, and/or shrimp) and combine with the clam. Add the crumbled bacon, bread crumbs, egg yolks, (no whites, yet!), poultry seasoning, parsley, garlic, Parmesan cheese, salt and pepper. Mix until thoroughly blended.

In a clean, dry, bowl, whip the egg whites using an electric beater until stiff peaks form. Fold the stiffened egg whites into the seafood mixture—don't overmix!

Scrub the clam shells thoroughly and arrange them on a lightly oiled cookie sheet. Brush the inside of each shell with a thin smear of butter. Evenly distribute the seafood mixture into the clam shells. Bake in a preheated oven set at 400 degrees for about half an hour or until the mixture has risen and is golden brown. Serve hot!

CONGER EEL COCKTAIL

Serves 4-6

I first learned of this unique preparation while fishing for cod aboard the STARSTREAM II out of Freeport, Long Island several years ago. Cod were scarce, but conger eels were abundant. The mates took a mess of eels into the cabin and on the trip home treated the passengers to this tasty appetizer.

2 lbs. conger eel fillets   **1/2 cup horseradish**
2 cups catsup

Cut the conger eel fillets into finger-size strips. Bring a saucepan of water to a boil. As soon as the water starts rolling, remove the pan from the heat and immediately put in the strips of conger eel. Cover the pan and set it aside for 5 minutes. Yes, the eel strips will cook thoroughly!

After 5 minutes, drain the eel strips and plunge them into a bowl of cold water for 10 minutes. Drain again and return the eel strips to the bowl. Add the catsup and horseradish and stir gently to mix. Chill and serve cold!

CRUNCHY CRAB NUGGETS

Serves 4-6

2 cups cooked crabmeat
2 eggs
1 cup bread crumbs
1 tablespoon finely minced
onion
1 tablespoon finely minced
celery

1/2 cup blanched walnut
meat, coarsely chopped
salt and pepper to taste
oil (enough for deep frying)

Flake the crabmeat into a bowl, then add the eggs, bread crumbs, onion, celery and walnut meat, and season with salt and pepper. Mix thoroughly.

Heat a large frypan and add enough oil for deep frying (about 3 inches). Shape the mixture into balls about the size of walnuts and fry in hot oil on all sides until golden brown. Drain and serve hot or cold!

FISH CAKES

Serves 4-6

1½ cups cooked, flaked
  codfish
1½ cups mashed potatoes
1 egg, beaten
1 tablespoon finely minced
  onion

1 tablespoon grated
  Parmesan cheese
salt and pepper to taste
flour
oil

In a large bowl, combine the flaked codfish, mashed potatoes, egg, onion, Parmesan cheese, salt and pepper. Mix until thoroughly blended, then chill in the refrigerator for about an hour.

Shape the mixture into patties and dredge in flour. Heat a large skillet then add enough oil to coat the bottom of the skillet. Fry the patties on both sides until golden brown. Drain and serve with a creamy sauce—I prefer SAUCE ROSA (see chapter 15).

FISH STICKS

1 lb. fluke fillets
1 egg, beaten
salt and pepper to taste

1 cup bread crumbs
oil (enough for deep frying)

Beat the eggs in a bowl, then season with salt and pepper. Pour the bread crumbs onto a plate.

Cut the fillets into strips of about 4 x ¾ inches. Dip the strips into the egg and roll in bread crumbs.

Heat a large frypan and add enough oil for deep frying (about 2 inches). Fry the fish sticks on both sides in the hot oil until golden brown. Drain. Serve hot or cold with tartar sauce and lemon wedges.

FISH-KEBOBS

Serves 4-6

1 lb. fish fillets (fluke, cod, sea bass, etc.)
1 bell pepper, cored, seeded and cut into chunks
1 cup firm pineapple chunks

1 large onion, cut into chunks
about 12 cherry tomatoes
oil

Cut the fillets into cubes. Alternately thread the fish cubes, pepper chunks, pineapple chunks, onion chunks and whole cherry tomatoes onto long, flat skewers. Brush evenly with oil.

Arrange the skewers on a broiling rack. Place the rack in a preheated broiler about 4 inches below the flame and broil for about 5 minutes on each side or until fish test done. Serve hot!

CRAB-STUFFED TOMATOES

Makes 4

**4 ripe beefsteak tomatoes
  (pick out large ones)
1 cup cooked crabmeat
1/2 cup cottage cheese**

**1/2 teaspoon finely
  chopped scallions
salt and pepper to taste**

Cut the top off each tomato, then carefully scoop out the meat without penetrating the outer skin. Chop the tomato pulp coarsely and place in a bowl. Add the crabmeat, cottage cheese and scallions. Season with salt and pepper, then mix until well blended. Spoon mixture into tomato shells. Chill and serve cold!

CHAPTER 14

SOUPS AND SALADS

by
AGLIANO

Sal

14

SOUPS AND SALADS

Many years ago while browsing through an Old World cookbook, I came upon an interesting bit of historical information tucked away in a footnote. The text at the bottom of the page described how many women of Eastern Europe, during a time of hardship and starvation, discovered a method of providing their very young with both nourishment and enough bulk to suppress the pangs of hunger by preparing a dish from leftover bones (from beef, lamb, fish, or whatever was available) and scraps of stale bread. The bones were boiled for hours in a large kettle filled with water, then the liquid was strained. Chunks of stale bread were added to the strained broth, pulverized into a pablum-like paste, and fed to the starving child. The preparation was appropriately called: SOUP OF A THOUSAND INFANTS!

This formula may have been the forerunner for many fancy soups, for bread is often used as a thickener. Soups range in consistency from light clear broths to thick, chunky chowders. Soups may also be thickened by flour, corn starch, a roux of flour and butter, or starchy vegetables such as potato or squash.

Similarly, many salads were constructed out of need and what was readily available. I recall my Uncle Tony Maccariello prowling the fields of Staten Island for dandelion greens and wild onions many years ago, then whipping up one of the tastiest salads I had ever had.

Nothing warms the body on a cold winter's day more than a bowl of piping hot soup. And nothing refreshes in the heat of summer more than a crisp, fresh salad. Both extremes of gastronomical pleasure are set forth in this chapter with the presence of fish or shellfish dominating each dish.

The following recipes provide a cross-section of several types of seafood soups.

PLAIN FISH BROTH

Serves 8-12

2 lbs. fish scraps (heads,
  tails, bones, skins and fins)
2 quarts water
2 carrots, cut into chunks
1 large onion, cut into chunks

2 celery ribs, cut into chunks
1 bay leaf
2 sprigs of fresh parsley
1 teaspoon thyme
salt and pepper to taste

Combine all ingredients in a large kettle and bring to a boil.
Lower flame to a simmer and cook gently for about 30
minutes. During cooking, use a slotted spoon to skim off the
scum as it rises until none is present. Strain the broth
through several layers of cheesecloth, discarding the fish
scraps and vegetables. Serve hot!

NEW ENGLAND STYLE CODFISH CHOWDER

Serves 8-12

2 lbs. codfish fillets
2 quarts FISH FUMET
  (see chapter 15)
1 cup diced salt pork (rinds
  removed)
1 medium-size onion, finely
  chopped

3 cups diced potato
3 tablespoons butter
2 cups half and half
salt and pepper to taste

Coarsely chop the codfish fillets and combine the fillets and the FISH FUMET in a large kettle. Simmer gently for about half an hour.

In a frypan, lightly brown the salt pork, add the onions and saute until the onions are limp. Add the pork pieces, onion and fat to the kettle. Add the potatoes and simmer for about 20 minutes or until potatoes are tender. Add the butter, half and half, salt and pepper. Simmer 5 minutes longer. Pour into a soup tureen and individual deep bowls. Serve piping hot with crackers.

MANHATTAN STYLE CODFISH CHOWDER

Serves 8-12

2 lbs. codfish fillets
2 quarts FISH FUMET
  (see chapter 15)
1 small onion, finely chopped
4 cups chopped tomatoes
4 celery ribs and leaves, diced

1/3 cup chopped fresh parsley
2 bay leaves
1 teaspoon thyme
3 cups diced potatoes
salt and pepper to taste
dash of Tabasco

Coarsely chop the codfish fillets and combine the fillets and the FISH FUMET in a large kettle. Simmer gently for half an hour. Add the onions, tomatoes, celery, carrots, parsley, bay leaves and thyme. Simmer gently for 15 minutes. After 15 minutes, add the potatoes, salt, pepper and Tabasco, and continue to simmer 20 minutes longer or until vegetables are tender. Pour into a soup tureen or individual bowls. Serve piping hot with crackers.

CODFISH CORN CHOWDER

Serves 8-12

2 lbs. codfish fillets
2 quarts FISH FUMET
  (see chapter 15)
1 small onion, diced
1 bell pepper, diced
2 cloves garlic, crushed

12 ears of corn
2 cups diced potatoes
1 pint heavy cream
2 tablespoons butter
salt and pepper to taste

Scrape the kernels from 10 ears of corn; cut the 2 remaining ears into 2-inch pieces. Set the kernels and the cut pieces of corn aside; don't discard the cobs. While preparing the FISH FUMET, add the cobs along with the fish scraps.

Coarsely chop the codfish fillets and combine the fillets and the FISH FUMET in a large kettle. Add the corn kernels, corn pieces and bell pepper; simmer gently for half an hour.

Add the onion, garlic and potatoes, and continue to simmer 20 minutes longer or until potatoes are tender. Add the butter, cream, salt and pepper, and simmer 5 minutes longer. Pour into a soup tureen or individual deep bowls. Serve piping hot with crackers.

ITALIAN SEAFOOD VEGETABLE SOUP

Serves 8-16

1 lb. medium shrimp, shelled and deveined
1 lb. squid, cleaned and cut into bite-size pieces
2 lbs. conger eel fillets, cut into strips
2 small onions, diced
2 cups chopped tomatoes
2 carrots, diced
1 zucchini, diced but not peeled
1/2 lb. Italian flat beans (or string beans)
1 cup diced celery
2 cups diced potatoes
1 cup raw long-grain rice
1 tablespoon butter
2 tablespoons olive oil
1 quart water
2 quarts chicken stock
1/2 cup fresh basil, torn into pieces
1 tablespoon chopped fresh parsley
1/8 teaspoon oregano
salt and pepper to taste

In a saucepan, gently simmer the squid pieces in 1 quart of water for about 40 minutes. Meanwhile, heat a large frypan and melt the butter. Just as the butter begins to foam add the olive oil, and when the oil is hot, add the onions, carrots, zucchini, string beans, celery and potatoes. Toss to evenly distribute vegetables. Cover the frypan, lower the flame and cook for about 5 minutes. Add the tomatoes, basil, parsley and oregano. Season with salt and pepper and simmer for about 20 minutes, stirring occasionally.

Pour the frypan contents into a large kettle. Add the chicken stock, the squid and the water the squid simmered in. Add the shrimp, conger eel strips and raw rice. Simmer gently for about 20 minutes or until the rice is tender. Serve in deep bowls. Sprinkle on some grated Parmesan cheese, and have some crusty Italian bread on the side. Serve piping hot!

SEA BASS TOMATO SOUP

Serves 8-12

4 lbs. ripe plum tomatoes
3 quarts FISH FUMET
  (see chapter 15)
1 lb. sea bass fillets
1/2 cup chili sauce
1/2 cup fresh basil, finely
  chopped

dashes of Worcestershire
  sauce and Tabasco
salt to taste
2 hard-boiled eggs

Core the tomatoes and make a shallow cross cut at the bottom of each tomato. Boil water in a large pot and put in the tomatoes. Boil for 2 minutes. Drain the tomatoes before plunging them into a bowl or pot of cold water (this loosens the skins and makes peeling easier). Peel the tomatoes and quarter them into a large kettle (don't lose any of the juices). Add the FISH FUMET and simmer gently for about an hour.

Working with small batches at a time, puree the tomatoes and broth in a food processor or blender. Return to the kettle.

Cut the fillets into chunks and add to the simmering stock with the chili sauce, basil, Worcestershire sauce and Tabasco. Season with salt and continue to simmer gently for about 30 minutes.

Pour the soup into individual deep bowls. Grate the hard-boiled eggs finely and use them to garnish the soup. Serve piping hot!

GARLIC SOUP WITH CRAB

Serves 8-12

The basis for this tasty soup comes from a classic Spanish dish called Sopa De Ajo (garlic soup). The soup is thickened with stale bread, and the addition of crab, although unfaithful to the original recipe, provides an interesting touch.

6 blue crabs, live
2 quarts water
4 cups stale Italian or French bread, cut into cubes

8-12 cloves garlic, whole
1/4 cup olive oil
1 teaspoon paprika
salt and pepper to taste

Stab kill the crabs, then remove the crabmeat and set aside in the refrigerator until ready to use. Discard the crab's gills and innards and crush the remaining shells, claws and swimmerettes in a large kettle. Add the 2 quarts of water and simmer gently for about half an hour. Strain the liquid through several layers of cheesecloth. Scrub the kettle to remove any particles of shell that may have stuck to the kettle. Return the crab-flavored stock to the kettle and simmer gently.

In a large frypan, heat the olive oil and saute the whole cloves of garlic until deep brown in color—don't burn them! Remove the garlic, mash into a paste and set aside. Fry the bread cubes until lightly browned. Remove the frypan from the heat and stir in the paprika. Add about a cup of the hot broth to the bread and mash the bread thoroughly. Stir in the mashed garlic.

Scrape the frypan contents into the kettle, add the crabmeat and season with salt and pepper. Simmer gently for 15 minutes, stirring frequently.

Pour the soup into a tureen or individual bowls and serve piping hot!

SEAFOOD AVOCADO BISQUE

Serves 8-12

1 cup cooked crabmeat
1 cup cooked lobster meat
1 cup poached baby shrimp
2 avocados, peeled and
  pitted

juice of 2 lemons
2 quarts chicken broth
1 cup heavy cream
1 tablespoon butter
salt and pepper to taste

Cut the avocados into chunks and pour on the lemon juice. Toss lightly then thoroughly mash the avocado.

In a large kettle, bring the chicken broth to a boil. Lower the flame, then add the mashed avocado, crabmeat, lobster meat and shrimp. Simmer for about 10 minutes, stirring continuously.

Add the cream, butter, salt and pepper, and continue to simmer for about 2 minutes. Serve piping hot with croutons or chilled with cucumber slices.

CARIBBEAN SEAFOOD CHOWDER   Serves 8-16

2 lbs. conch, cleaned with viscera removed
1 lb. squid, cleaned and cut into bite-size pieces
1 lb. fish fillets (cod, flounder, sea bass, etc.)
12 mussels, live
12 little neck clams, live
3 quarts water
juice of 1 large orange
juice of 1/2 lime
1 cup diced salt pork (rinds removed)
3 large onions, diced
1 green bell pepper, cored, seeded and diced
1 red bell pepper, cored, seeded and diced
1 yellow bell pepper, cored, seeded and diced
4 cloves garlic, crushed
3 potatoes, peeled and diced
1 teaspoon thyme
1 bay leaf
1/2 cup parsley
1 tablespoon Tabasco
salt to taste

Pound the conch flat with a wooden mallet, then cut the meat into strips. In a bowl, combine the conch strips, squid pieces, orange juice and lime juice. Toss lightly then set aside at room temperature for about 30 minutes.

After 30 minutes, combine the conch, squid, fruit juices and 3 quarts of water in a large kettle. Bring to a boil then lower flame and simmer gently for about an hour.

While the conch and squid are simmering, fry the salt pork in a large frypan. When the pork pieces begin to brown, remove them and set aside. To the fat in the frypan, add the onions, bell peppers and garlic. Saute until the vegetables are limp. After the conch and squid have simmered for an hour, add the frypan ingredients to the kettle with the fried salt pork, diced potatoes, thyme, bay leaf and Tabasco. Season with salt. Continue simmering.

Scrub clean the mussels and clams and debeard the mussels. As soon as the cleaning is done, add the shellfish to the kettle. Cut the fillets into chunks and also add to the kettle. Simmer for about 20 minutes or until potatoes are tender. Stir in the parsley, then pour the chowder into a soup tureen or into individual deep bowls. Serve piping hot!

AUTUMN HARVEST SOUP

Serves 8-12

1 lb. blackfish fillets
3 quarts FISH FUMET
(see chapter 15)
8 cups fresh pumpkin meat
2 cloves garlic, crushed
2 ribs fennel, diced
1 medium-size zucchini,
diced but not peeled

1 teaspoon chopped
coriander leaves
salt and pepper to taste
1 pint heavy cream
2 tablespoons butter

Hollow a fresh pumpkin and combine 8 cups of pumpkin meat and the FISH FUMET in a large kettle (set hollowed pumpkin aside to be used as a soup tureen). Simmer gently for about 45 minutes, stirring gently. Strain the cooked pumpkin and return the stock to the kettle. In a food processor or using a potato masher, reduce the pumpkin meat to a puree. Return the mashed pumpkin to the kettle, then add the garlic, fennel, zucchini, coriander, salt and pepper. Simmer for about 15 minutes or until vegetables are slightly tender.

Cut the blackfish fillets into chunks and add to the kettle along with the cream and butter. Simmer gently for half an hour. Pour the soup into the hollowed out pumpkin—just make sure the pumpkin is flat-bottomed so it won't tip over or leak! Serve piping hot!

PLAIN CRAB SALAD

Serves 4-6

2 cups cooked crabmeat
1 tablespoon finely diced
  onion
1 tablespoon finely diced
  celery

juice of 1/2 lemon
1 cup mayonnaise
  (see chapter 15)
salt and white pepper
  to taste

Flake crabmeat in a bowl. Add the onion, celery and lemon juice. Season with salt and pepper and toss lightly. Add the mayonnaise and fold into the crab until the ingredients are well blended. Pack the mixture, cover with plastic wrap and chill in the refrigerator for about an hour.

Serve over a bed of lettuce or as a sandwich spread.

NOTE: lobster or shrimp may be substituted for the crab. Or you may want to combine crab, shrimp and/or lobster (2 cups total) for a mixed seafood salad.

CRAB WALDORF

Serves 4-6

2 cups cooked crabmeat
1/2 cup finely diced celery
one of each: apple, pear,
   orange
12-16 seedless grapes,
   mixed varieties

juice of 1 lemon
1/4 cup blanched walnuts,
   broken into small pieces
1 cup mayonnaise
   (see chapter 15)
2 tablespoons heavy cream

Core, peel and cut the apple and pear into 1/2-inch cubes. Place into a large bowl, pour on the lemon juice and toss. Peel the orange and divide into sections. Add the orange sections to the apple and pear. Add the celery, grapes and walnut pieces.

In a small bowl, combine the mayonnaise and heavy cream. Whip until smooth. Add the crabmeat and stir in. Pour the crab mixture over the prepared fruits and fold in gently until well blended. Chill for an hour.

SEAFOOD AVOCADO SALAD

Serves 4-6

2 avocados
juice of 1 lemon
1/2 cup cooked crabmeat
1/4 cup cooked baby shrimp
1 tablespoon green olives,
  pitted and chopped

1 tablespoon black olives,
  pitted and chopped
1 teaspoon roasted
  peppers, finely chopped
1 cup sour cream (or plain
  yogurt)

Cut the avocados in half and remove the pits. Brush the lemon juice over the flesh of the avocados, then chill briefly in the refrigerator.

While the avocados are chilling, flake the crabmeat into a bowl. Add the shrimp, green and black olives, roasted peppers and sour cream. Mix until well blended.

Spoon the mixture into the pit cavity of the avocados. Sprinkle a dash of cayenne pepper over each. Serve chilled!

HOMEMADE TUNA SALAD

Serves 4-6

Once you savor this tasty salad, you'll never go back to canned tuna. You must, of course, hook into an albacore—not bonito or false albacore, but the long-finned tackle-buster. Butcher the fish however you like, but save one steak for HOMEMADE TUNA SALAD!

1 albacore steak
   (about 8 ounces)
1/2 quart COURT BOUILLON
   (see chapter 15)
1 tablespoon finely diced
   onion
1 tablespoon finely diced
   celery

1 tablespoon finely diced
   bell pepper
juice of 1 lemon
1 cup OLIVE OIL
   MAYONNAISE
   (see chapter 15)
salt and white pepper
   to taste

Trim the tuna steak of bones and skin. Place the trimmed tuna into a saucepan, cover with 1/2 quart of COURT BOUILLON and simmer gently for about 20 minutes. Drain the tuna and discard the liquid. Flake the tuna in a medium-size bowl, cover with plastic wrap and chill for about an hour.

After an hour, combine the tuna with the onion, celery and bell pepper. Add the lemon juice and toss lightly. Add the OLIVE OIL MAYONNAISE, season with salt and pepper and mix until blended. Chill again then serve on a bed of lettuce or as sandwich spread!

SCUNGILLI SALAD

Serves 4-6

2 conch, shelled and
  viscera removed
2 cups iceberg lettuce
  hearts, coarsely chopped

juice of 2 lemons
4-6 cloves garlic, sliced
1 tablespoon olive oil
salt and pepper to taste

Pound the conch flat with a wooden mallet then cut into strips. Bring water to a boil, then lower flame and add the conch. Simmer for about an hour or until conch are tender. Drain and chill. Place the chilled conch into a bowl and pour on the lemon juice. Toss lightly. Add the lettuce hearts, garlic, salt, pepper and olive oil. Toss to mix. Serve chilled!

SEA MONSTER SALAD Serves 4-8

1 lb. small squid, cleaned and cut into bite-size pieces

1 lb. small octopi, cleaned and cut into bite-size pieces

1 lb. conger eel fillets, cut into strips

1 quart water

1 tablespoon red wine vinegar

4 cloves garlic, sliced

1 red onion, sliced paper-thin

1 cup VINAIGRETTE (see chapter 15)

In a medium-size saucepan, bring the water and vinegar to a boil. Lower the flame and add the conger eel strips. Simmer gently for 5 minutes—no longer! Scoop out the eel strips, drain and chill until ready to use.

In the same water used to simmer the conger eels, simmer the squid and octopi for about 2 minutes or until tender. Drain and discard the liquid. Chill the squid and octopi in the refrigerator for about half an hour.

In a large bowl, toss together the squid, octopi and conger eel. Add the sliced raw garlic, toss lightly, then spread the mixture onto a large platter. Separate the sliced onion into rings and distribute over the seafood. Cover with plastic wrap and chill. Just before serving pour on the VINAIGRETTE.

NOTE: cooking squid and octopus is tricky business. If you cook just a fraction too long, they will become tough again. To correct, you must continue to cook for about an hour to tenderize again. CHECK OFTEN FOR DONENESS!

CODFISH AND ARTICHOKE SALAD

Serves 4-6

2 lbs. codfish fillets
4 small artichokes
2 cloves garlic, minced
 finely

1/4 cup olive oil
salt and white pepper to
 taste

In a saucepan, poach the codfish fillets in water until done (about 10 minutes). Drain the codfish and flake into a bowl. Chill until ready to use.

Trim the spiny ends from the artichoke leaves and cut off the stems. Bring water to a boil in the bottom half of the steamer (do not use aluminum, it will darken the artichokes). When steam fills the upper chamber, place the artichokes into the upper chamber, sprinkle on the garlic, cover and steam cook for about 40 minutes or until artichokes are tender. Drain and chill.

Carefully pull the artichoke leaves away from the base; set leaves aside. Chop the artichokes hearts coarsely and toss with the flaked codfish. Add the olive oil, salt and pepper, and toss. Spread the mixture over a large serving platter. Arrange the artichoke leaves around the border of the platter. Serve chilled.

GREEK STYLE
CODFISH SALAD

Serves 4-8

2 lbs. codfish fillets
2 ripe plum tomatoes,
  cored and quartered
1 cup Greek olives
2 cloves garlic, sliced
1/4 lb. Feta cheese,
  crumbled

1 tablespoon chopped fresh
  parsley
4 scallions, sliced
1/8 teaspoon oregano
1/2 cup olive oil
salt and pepper to taste
1 head Romaine lettuce

Poach the codfish gently in water until done (about 10 minutes). Drain and flake the codfish into a large bowl. Chill for about 15 minutes.

Combine all the ingredients except the lettuce with the codfish and toss to mix thoroughly. Tear apart the lettuce leaves and drape them over a large serving platter. Spread the codfish mixture over the lettuce. Serve chilled!

CHRISTMAS EVE SEAFOOD SALAD

Serves 6-12

Every Christmas Eve my wife and my mother go all out to collaborate on this special traditional holiday dish. Preparations are somewhat involved, but the end result justifies the extra effort.

1 lb. codfish fillets
1 lb. squid, cleaned and viscera removed
1 lb. conch, shelled and viscera removed
2 cups baby shrimp
1 cup celery, finely diced
1 cup stuffed, Spanish olives, sliced

1 cup black olives, pitted and sliced
4-8 cloves garlic, sliced
juice of 2 lemons
3/4 cup olive oil
pepper to taste
salt to taste (optional)

Cut the squid hoods into rings and the tentacles into bite-size pieces. Pound the conch with a wooden mallet and cut into strips.

In individual pots of water, poach the codfish, squid, conch and shrimp until done and tender (refer to Chapter 2 for proper cooking time). Drain the fish and shellfish, then flake the codfish and combine all cooked seafood in a large bowl. Toss lightly then chill for about an hour.

After an hour, add to the seafood the celery, Spanish olives, black olives, garlic and lemon juice; toss lightly. Add the olive oil, pepper and salt (taste before adding salt, the olives and celery usually provide enough salt to season the dish). Toss to mix. Serve chilled.

SEAFOOD COLESLAW Serves 6-12

1 1-lb. cabbage, cored and
  shredded
1 carrot, peeled and
  shredded
1 small onion, finely minced
2 green bell peppers
1 cup mayonnaise
  (see chapter 15)

1 teaspoon sugar
1 cup cooked crabmeat,
  flaked
1 cup cooked lobster meat,
  coarsely chopped
1 cup cooked baby shrimp
salt and pepper to taste

In a very large bowl, combine the shredded cabbage, shredded carrot and onion. Core one pepper and remove the seeds and membrane; dice finely. Add the diced pepper to the cabbage mixture. Toss lightly.

Add the mayonnaise, sugar, crab, lobster and shrimp. Season with salt and pepper and toss until ingredients are well blended and distributed. Cover with plastic wrap and chill in the refrigerator for about an hour.

After chilling, spread the mixture onto a serving platter. Core and remove the seeds and membrane from the bell pepper. Slice the pepper into 1/4-inch rings and use to decorate the SEAFOOD COLESLAW. Serve chilled.

SEAFOOD MACARONI SALAD

Serves 6-12

1 lb. macaroni (pasta)
1 cup cooked crabmeat,
  flaked
1 cup cooked lobster meat,
  coarsely chopped
1 cup cooked baby shrimp
1/2 cup green olives, pitted
  and sliced
1/2 cup roasted peppers,
  coarsely chopped
1 tablespoon blanched
  pine nuts
1 cup mayonnaise
  (see chapter 15)
1 cup finely minced onion
salt and pepper to taste

Cook the pasta in lightly salted water until tender. Drain and chill for about an hour. (If you mix about a tablespoon of oil to the drained pasta before chilling, it will prevent sticking.)

Place the chilled pasta in a large bowl. Add the crabmeat, lobster, shrimp, green olives and roasted peppers. Toss lightly.

Crush the pine nuts in a mortar and pestle (or in a bowl with the back of a spoon) until roughly crumbled. Add to the pasta and seafood and toss. Add the mayonnaise, onion, salt and pepper. Mix until thoroughly blended. Transfer to a serving platter, cover with plastic wrap and chill for about an hour before serving.

SEAFOOD POTATO SALAD

Serves 6-12

2 lbs. potatoes, peeled and
cut into 1/4-inch slices
1 cup cooked crabmeat
1 cup cooked lobster meat,
coarsely chopped
1 cup cooked baby shrimp
4 slices bacon
2 hard-boiled eggs, peeled
and quartered

2 cups sour cream (or plain
yogurt)
1 small onion, minced
finely
salt and pepper to taste
paprika

Boil the potato slices in lightly salted water until tender—not mushy! Drain the potatoes and soak in cold water until ready to use.

Fry the bacon until crisp. Drain thoroughly on paper towels then crumble into a small bowl; set aside.

Drain the potatoes and gently pat dry. Place the potatoes in a large bowl. Add the crabmeat, lobster, shrimp, onion and sour cream. Season with salt and pepper and toss until well blended. Pour the potato and seafood mixture onto a large platter. Arrange the egg sections over the potato salad and sprinkle on the crumbled bacon. Dust lightly with paprika. Cover with plastic wrap and chill for about an hour before serving.

CHAPTER 15

THE SAUCE MAKES THE DIFFERENCE!

by
AGLIANO

Sal

COOKING·WITH
Sal

15
THE SAUCE MAKES THE DIFFERENCE

I must have been about 10 years old before I realized there were sauces other than the thick, rich homemade tomato sauce my grandmother Luisa prepared and jarred in our kitchen year after year.

Each year after the summer, several bushels of fresh, ripe plum tomatoes arrived at our doorstep. This was the impetus for a two-day ritual of jar-cleaning, tomato-trimming, boiling, straining, seasoning, and finally jarring enough tomato sauce to last throughout the winter, spring, and summer months.

Luisa, my mother, Michelina, my brother, Stephen (who was a mere tot at the time), and I sat around the bushels of tomatoes, washing, coring, and quartering. The tomatoes were heaped into several large kettles, seasoned then simmered for hours.

Then came the part I enjoyed most—operating the steel grinding machine which separated the pulp from the skin and seeds. I turned the crank while Luisa poured the hot tomato mixture into the funneled hopper. The mixture would pass through a perforated tube, pressing the pulp through the holes and ejecting the skin and seeds through the end opening of the tube.

Mom and Granma sterilized the jays, sealing rings, caps, and rubber gaskets. The mixture was divided among the jars and then my brother, Steve, performed his favorite task of placing a fresh basil leaf into each jar. We used an immense two-burner galvanized basin to complete the job by boiling the sealed jars for preserving. When done, the jars of homemade tomato sauce were stored on shelves in our pantry for the duration.

Although Grandma Luisa's rich tomato sauce will always have a special place in my heart, there are other fine sauces that can be whipped up in a wink right on the stovetop. Sometimes all it takes is a light application of sauce to make the difference between a dull, run-of-the-mill dish and a truly fascinating dining experience. This final chapter deals exclusively with just such a notion—sauces which enhance and complement the flavor of those finny creatures and crawling invertebrates we so enjoy eating!

FISH FUMET

This clear broth is the basis from which many flavorful sauces are prepared (makes about 2 quarts).

4 lbs. fish scraps (heads, tails, bones, skin, and fins)
4 quarts cold water

Clean the fish scraps of any trace of viscera and gills (these are inedible and should not be used in cooking). Score the head and break the bones to fit into a large kettle. Pour 4 quarts of water over the fish scraps and boil vigorously for about half an hour or until the liquid is reduced by half. With a slotted spoon, skim off any scum which rises to the surface until none appears. Strain the liquid through cheesecloth. Discard scraps.

COURT BOUILLON

This is a light vegetable broth used primarily for poaching. It may also be used as a starter for other sauces. (Makes about 2 quarts).

1 large onion, quartered
1 large carrot, cut into chunks
2 leeks, cut into chunks
1 celery rib, cut into chunks
4 cloves garlic, crushed
1 cup chopped fresh
   parsley

2 bay leaves
1 teaspoon thyme
1 teaspoon salt
4 peppercorns, crushed
1½ quarts cold water
2 cups dry white wine

In a large kettle, combine all the ingredients and simmer gently for 30 minutes. Strain the liquid through cheesecloth and discard the vegetables.

FISH COURT BOUILLON

1 quart fish fumet

1 cup court bouillon

Combine the strained court bouillon in a large kettle. Simmer until hot, stirring occasionally. (Makes about 2 quarts).

BASIC ROUX

This is a basic thickening formula into which flavored broths are stirred to create a variety of fish sauces.

4 tablespoons butter   **4 tablespoons flour**

In a medium-size saucepan, melt the butter then stir in the flour. Lower the flame and continue to cook while stirring vigorously until mixture begins to bubble (about 5 minutes). Some roux are allowed to cook longer to produce various shades of brown. However, the longer you cook the roux, the less effective the thickening powers become. Also used to thicken soups and chowders.

LEMON ROUX

4 tablespoons butter   **juice of 1 lemon, strained**
4 tablespoons flour

This is a variation of the above recipe. Prepare the same as BASIC ROUX, then stir in the lemon juice until well blended.

VELOUTE SAUCE

(Makes about 1/2 quart)

4 tablespoons butter
4 tablespoons flour

4 cups FISH FUMET,
    COURT BOUILLON OR
    FISH BOUILLON

Melt the butter in a medium-size saucepan, then add the flour. Lower the flame and continue to cook while stirring vigorously with a wire whisk until the mixture begins to bubble. Remove the pan from the heat and pour in the FISH FUMET or COURT BOUILLON (the stock should be hot). Whisk vigorously until the mixture is smooth and creamy. Return to the heat and continue to cook for about 5 minutes, stirring continously, until the sauce has thickened to desired consistency. Great for poached or baked fish or shellfish.

BECHAMEL SAUCE

This all-purpose sauce is frequently used as a starter for some of the grandest seafood toppings. Also great by itself without any embellishments. (Makes about 1/2 quart).

4 tablespoons butter
4 tablespoons flour
3 cups hot milk

1 cup heavy cream
salt and white pepper to taste
pinch of nutmeg

Prepare a roux using butter and flour. When the mixture begins to bubble, remove from heat and pour in the hot milk. Stir vigorously until mixture is smooth and creamy. Return to the heat and cook for about 3 minutes stirring continuously. Remove from the heat and add the salt, pepper and nutmeg. Pour in the heavy cream and stir vigorously until smooth and creamy. Great for poached or baked fish. This is also the thickening agent for souffles and pot pies.

SAUCE MORNAY

2 cups BECHAMEL SAUCE
3 tablespoons Gruyere
cheese, grated
2 tablespoons Parmesan
cheese, grated

1 tablespoon butter
1/2 cup heavy cream

Add the Gruyere and Parmesan cheese to hot BECHAMEL SAUCE and cook over a very low flame until the cheeses have melted. Remove from heat and add the butter and heavy cream. Whip until well blended. (Makes about 3 cups).

SAUCE ROSA

No, this sauce wasn't named after a girl called Rosie! It is so called because of the rose-colored effect of the tomato.

2 cups BECHAMEL SAUCE   **2 tablespoons tomato puree**
4 hard-boiled eggs,
   coarsely, chopped

Prepare the BECHAMEL SAUCE, then stir in the tomato puree and cook briefly over a low flame. Remove from the heat and stir in the chopped eggs. (Makes about 3 cups).

HOLLANDAISE SAUCE

Ah! The classic sauce for Eggs Benedict! Also great for seafood.

6 egg yolks   **1 teaspoon salt**
2 tablespoons cold water   **1/2 teaspoon white pepper**
1 lb. butter, cut into chips   **juice of 1 lemon, strained**

Bring water to a boil in the bottom half of a double boiler. Lower the flame to a gentle simmer, then insert the upper chamber of the double boiler. Pour into the upper chamber the egg yolks and the cold water. Whisk continuously until smooth. Add the butter, one chip at a time, stirring continuously until all the butter has been used and the sauce is smooth. Add the salt, pepper and lemon juice, and continue to cook while beating until the sauce is thick and creamy. Try on poached or baked fish. (Makes about 2 cups). NOTE: to achieve perfection never allow the water to boil. Slow cooking is the secret!

BEARNAISE SAUCE

1 cup dry white wine
1/2 cup cider vinegar
2 cloves garlic, finely
  minced
1 scallion, finely chopped
6 egg yolks

1 lb. butter, cut into chips
1 tablespoon chopped
  tarragon
1 teaspoon finely chopped
  parsley
salt and pepper to taste

In a small frypan, heat the wine, vinegar, garlic and scallion to a boil. Lower the flame and simmer gently until the liquid is reduced to a syrup. Strain the liquid into a bowl, pressing out as much juice as possible.

Bring water to a boil in the bottom half of a double boiler. Lower the flame to a gentle simmer, then insert the upper chamber of the double boiler. Pour in the reserved liquid and the egg yolks. Whisk continuously until smooth. Add the butter, one chip at a time, stirring continuously until all the butter has been used. Add the tarragon, parsley, salt and pepper, and continue to simmer, while stirring, until sauce is thick and creamy. (Makes about 2 cups).

BUERRE BLANC
(white butter sauce)

1 cup dry white wine
3/4 cup white vinegar
2 scallions, finely chopped

1 clove garlic, finely minced
1 lb. butter, cut into chips
salt and pepper to taste

In a frypan, heat the wine, vinegar, scallions and garlic until most of the liquid has evaporated. Lower the flame to a gentle simmer, then add the butter, one chip at a time, stirring continuously until all the butter has been used and the mixture is creamy. Remove from the heat and stir in the salt and pepper. Great for baked or broiled fish or shellfish. (Makes about 2 cups).

BUERRE NOIR
(black butter sauce)

1 lb. butter
2 tablespoons capers

3 tablespoons parsley
1 tablespoon white vinegar

Soak the capers in warm water for about 15 minutes, then drain. In a saucepan, melt the butter over high heat until it turns a deep brown. Immediately add the capers, parsley and vinegar. Stir in briefly, then remove from the heat. Pour over baked, poached, broiled or grilled fish. (Makes about 1 quart).

SAUCE ROUILLE

The final accompaniment to BOUILLABAISE, this spicy garlic mayonnaise may be used to flavor poached fish.

4 cloves garlic
1 egg yolk
1/4 teaspoon cayenne pepper

pinch of saffron
salt to taste
1/2 cup olive oil

Crush the garlic into a paste, then add the egg yolk and beat in until well blended. Pour mixture into a mixing bowl and with a hand-held electric mixer, beat until egg is creamy. Add the cayenne pepper, saffron and salt. A teaspoon at a time, dribble in the olive oil in a steady stream until all the oil has been used and the sauce is smooth and creamy. (Makes about 3/4 cup).

TRADITIONAL MAYONNAISE

Once you savor this homemade blend, you'll never again settle for the store-bought mayonnaise. The secret to preparing mayonnaise is to have the ingredients at room temperature and to slowly dribble in the oil. Stored in a tightly covered container in the refrigerator, mayonnaise will keep for several days.

4 egg yolks
1/2 tablespoon white vinegar
juice of 1 lemon, strained
1/8 teaspoon dry mustard
dash of paprika
2 cups oil
salt and white pepper to taste

Place the egg yolks in a mixing bowl, then with a hand-held electric mixer, beat the yolks until smooth. Add the vinegar, lemon juice, dry mustard, paprika, salt and pepper, and continue to mix. Using a measuring device, dribble in the oil, one tablespoonful at a time, until all the oil has been used and the mayonnaise is smooth and creamy. (Makes about 2 cups).

OLIVE OIL MAYONNAISE

This is a slightly different approach to preparing mayonnaise. The initial flavoring of the oil should be done about a week ahead.

2 cups olive oil
2 cloves garlic, crushed
1 teaspoon crush tarragon
4 egg yolks

1/2 teaspoon white vinegar
juice of 1 lemon, strained
salt and white pepper to
** taste**

Place the crushed garlic and tarragon in a one-quart jar with a tight-fitting lid. Pour the olive oil over the garlic and tarragon, secure the lid and set aside in a dark place for about a week.

After a week, strain the olive oil and discard the garlic and tarragon. Place the egg yolks in a mixing bowl, then beat until smooth with an electric mixer. Add the vinegar, mayonnaise, salt and pepper. Continue to mix. Dribble in the flavored oil, one tablespoon at a time, until all the oil has been used and the mayonnaise is smooth and creamy. Great for poached cold fish or as a basting mixture for baked fillets. (Makes about 2 cups).

HOMEMADE TARTAR SAUCE #1

This is the traditional formula for TARTAR SAUCE. Again, I must say that after savoring the homemade batch, the store-bought variety will become only a dull memory.

2 cups TRADITIONAL MAYONNAISE
2 dill pickles, finely chopped
1 teaspoon finely minced onion
1/2 teaspoon anchovy paste
1 teaspoon finely chopped capers
1/2 teaspoon sugar

Combine all the ingredients in a large bowl and stir until well blended. That's all it takes! Great for deep fried fish or shellfish. A grand topping for deep fried soft shell crabs! (Makes about 2 cups).

HOMEMADE TARTAR SAUCE #2

This is a sweeter version of the above recipe. The kiddies go wild over this one!

2 cups TRADITIONAL MAYONNAISE
4 sweet gherkins, finely chopped
1 tablespoon finely minced onion
1 teaspoon finely minced green bell pepper
1 teaspoon finely minced red bell pepper

Combine all ingredients in a large bowl and stir until well blended. (Makes about 2 cups).

NOTE: I prefer tartar sauce to be as thick as mayonnaise, but if you insist on a thinner sauce, add 1/2 cup heavy cream and stir until smooth.

VINAIGRETTE

This light sauce is primarily used for cold fish or shellfish in salads. It may also be used as a marinade for baked, broiled, or steamed fish.

3/4 cup olive oil
1/3 cup red wine vinegar
1 teaspoon salt
1/2 teaspoon white pepper
1/8 teaspoon dill
1/2 teaspoon chopped fresh
  parsley

Combine the salt, pepper and vinegar in a bowl. Whisk until the salt has dissolved. Add the dill and parsley and stir briefly. Pour in the olive oil, then transfer the mixture to a jar or container with a tight-fitting lid. Shake until well blended. (Makes about 1 cup).

SCAMPI SAUCE

This is my favorite topping for baked or broiled fish and especially broiled shellfish. I also enjoy SCAMPI SAUCE poured over a side dish of pasta served with broiled shrimp.

1 lb. butter
juice of 1 lemon
4 cloves garlic, finely
  minced
1/4 cup chopped fresh
  parsley
salt and pepper to taste

In a frypan, soften the butter into a liquid over very low heat. Skim off the solid foam which will rise to the top of the butter (you have now clarified the butter). Add the garlic and saute lightly. Remove the frypan from the heat and stir in the remaining ingredients. Pour hot over baked, broiled, or poached fish or shellfish. (Makes about 3/4 cup).

SKORTHALIA or SKORDALIA

The Greeks call this pungent garlic sauce SKORTHALIA, and in the Middle East it is referred to as SKORDALIA. By whichever name, it is a super dipping sauce not only for deep-fried fish or shellfish, but also for breaded fried vegetables. I also enjoy it in salads. The sauce can be as mild or as powerful as you prefer—it all depends on how much garlic you use!

4 medium-size potatoes
2 slices white bread, trimmed
  of crusts and cubed
8-24 cloves garlic
  (12 is average)
1/2 cup red wine vinegar

2 cups olive oil
pinch of oregano
salt and pepper to taste
1/2 teaspoon lemon juice
water (as needed)

Peel and dice the potatoes, then boil in a pot of water until soft. Drain the potatoes and toss in a bowl about a spoonful of olive oil. Chill until ready to use.

Place the bread cubes in a large bowl. Add the garlic, wine vinegar, olive oil, oregano, salt, pepper and lemon juice. Press the mixture together into a ball and set aside for about 5 minutes.

Pour the bread mixture into a food processor and blend at high speed until the mixture rolls along the sides of the bowl. Add the potatoes and blend again until thoroughly mixed. Change the speed to the lowest setting and dribble in water until desired consistency is reached—the sauce should be smooth but slightly thick. Transfer the garlic sauce to a bowl, cover with plastic wrap and chill overnight. Just before serving, beat the sauce vigorously. Serve in a side bowl for dipping! (Makes about 3 cups).

FOUR "Cs" and a "P"

More of a basting mixture than a sauce, this blend was originally used for baked fowl. When I applied it to seafood, I discovered a new method for preparing some of my favorite dishes. The letters in the recipe title refer to the spices used: cinnamon, cumin, cloves, coriander and paprika (four Cs and a P).

1/4 lb. butter
1 teaspoon cinnamon
1 teaspoon ground cumin
1/2 teaspoon ground cloves

1/2 teaspoon ground
  coriander seeds
1 teaspoon paprika
salt and pepper to taste

Soften butter slightly—just enough to blend in the spices. Add the spices, salt and pepper, and stir until smooth and well blended. Brush mixture over fillets, shrimp or scallops as a basting for a baked or broiled fish. This batch is enough for 2 lbs. of fish or shellfish.

QUICK COCKTAIL SAUCE

2 cups catsup   **1/2 cup horseradish**

Mix the catsup and horseradish until well blended. Chill and stir into boiled, chilled shrimp or cooked cold fish cubes. (Makes about 2½ cups).

DIJON BUTTER SAUCE

1/4 lb. butter   **1/4 teaspoon dill**
3 teaspoons Dijon mustard   **salt and pepper to taste**
1 teaspoon lemon juice

Soften the butter enough to mix into the other ingredients. Add the mustard, lemon juice, dill, salt and pepper. Whip until smooth. Chill before using. Spread over poached hot or cold fish. (Makes about 3/4 cup).

SEAFOOD PASTA SAUCE

I could easily have devoted an entire chapter to the preparation of the many variations of pasta seafood sauces. However, each evolved from one basic formula. The differences lie in when to add the seafood.

3 tablespoons olive oil
4 cloves garlic, crushed
3 28-oz. cans crushed
   tomatoes (or about 6 lbs.
   ripe plum tomatoes,
   cored and peeled)

4-6 leaves torn, fresh basil
1 teaspoon chopped fresh
   parsley
1 cup dry white wine
salt and pepper to taste

In a very large kettle, heat the olive oil then lightly saute the garlic. Add the crushed tomatoes (or fresh tomatoes, smashed, with their juices), tomato paste, basil, parsley and wine. Simmer gently over a very low flame for 2½ to 3 hours; stir frequently. When done add the salt and pepper. (Makes about 2 quarts).

SEAFOOD ADDITIONS:

Clams and/or mussels—scrub the clams and mussels and debeard the mussels. Hold off adding the wine to the sauce, instead pour it over the clams and/or mussels lined in the bottom of a large pot. Cover the pot and boil rapidly for about 3 minutes or until the shellfish shells have opened. Discard those clams or mussels which failed to open their shells. About an hour before the sauce is done, add the shellfish (with or without the shells—the choice is yours) and the wine. The wine should be strained.

Shrimp or scallops—shell and devein the shrimps then add the shrimps and/or scallops about an hour before the sauce is done. A variation is to bread the shrimp or scallops and deep fry them before adding them to the sauce about 15 minutes before the sauce is done.

Crabs or lobsters—stab kill the crabs or lobsters, clean and cut into sections. Add to the sauce an hour before the sauce is done.

Squid, octopus, or conch—clean, cut into bite-size pieces and add to the sauce as soon as all the other ingredients have been assembled. Should cook for at least an hour and a half.

Fish fillets—whole fish fillets may be added about three-quarters of an hour before the sauce is done. Care should be exercised in stirring to avoid breaking the fillets apart. Cubed fish may be added about half an hour before the sauce is done.

Black eels—skin and gut the eels, then cut into 1-inch pieces. Add to the sauce about one and a half hours before the sauce is done.

Any combinations of fish and shellfish may be added to produce a rich and tasty SEAFOOD PASTA SAUCE, just introduce them at the appropriate time.

ABOUT THE AUTHOR

Sal Agliano began fishing at eight years old using a tree limb, string and a bent pin for a hook. At 14 he was renting skiffs in Sheepshead Bay and later spent more than 20 years learning the ropes on Captain Paul Luisa's charter boat the "Sailfin" out of Mill Basin in Brooklyn.

Perched on a kitchen chair Sal watched his mom, Michelena, and grandmother, Luisa, cook the daily meals. It was only natural that cooking and recipes became a big part of his life. Sal's professional cooking career started as a short order cook. Today he is Regional Manager for Tombrook Corporation, involved in menu planning and creating new dishes. His culinary work has taken him from Florida to Massachusetts.

Veteran outdoor scribe and friend, Matt Ahern, helped Sal get started writing fishing stories and recipes for THE FISHERMAN, much to the enjoyment of the publication's readers. A course from The Institute of Childrens Learning got Sal off on writing childrens stories for such magazines as HIGHLIGHTS FOR CHILDREN, AIM, CLUBHOUSE, THE FRIEND, JUNIOR TRAILS and RANGER RICK. One of his short stories is used in the anthology. "First-Time Authors" for the Institute of Childrens Literature study course material.

Sal Agliano still resides in Brooklyn, fishes often and writes the "Captain's Table" series for THE FISHERMAN.